Landmark

Flc

The

G000154866

Don Philpott

Dedicated to my beautiful American rose

Don Philpott is a journalist, author and broadcaster who has spent the last thirty years exploring the world as a writer. Born in Hull, England, he worked for twenty years with the Press Association, the UK national news agency. He founded and co-edited Footloose, an outdoor activities magazine in the UK.

He now lives in Florida and heads an international communications company. He has written more than 55 books on travel, wine, food, diet and health issues and the media.

Published by

Landmark Publishing

Ashbourne Hall, Cokayne Ave, Ashbourne,
Derbyshire DE6 1EJ England

Jet ski rental hire, Long Key

Landmark Visitors Guide

Florida:
The Keys

Don Philpott

Introduction   6

Geography   7
Getting there   8
A Brief History   9
Weather   16
The People   17
Flora and Fauna   17
Food and Drink   21
Sports and
   Pastimes   24
Classification of
   the Keys   26

1. Upper Keys 27

Key Largo   27
Map of Key Largo   30
Eating out on
   Key Largo   36/37
Islamorada or
The Purple Isles   39
Map of Islamorada   39
Eating out on
   Islamorada   48/49

2. Middle and Lower Keys   51

Middle Keys   51
Map of Marathon   54
Eating out on
   Marathon &
   Middle Keys   60/61
Map of Lower
   Keys   62
Lower Keys   63
Eating out on the
   Lower Keys   69

3. Key West   70

Map of Key West   71
Map of Key West,
   Old Town   77
Places of Interest   80
Key West
   Festivals   99
Eating out on
   Key West   100/101

FactFile 102

Before you go 102
Accommodation 104
Airports 131
Airlines 131
Alcohol 131
Babysitting 131
Banks 132
Bicycles 132
Bus 132
Camping/Recreational
  Vehicles 132
Car Rental
  Companies 135
Clothing and Packing 136
Currency 136
Disabled 137
Diving 137
Driving on the Keys 139
Electricity 143
Embassies and
  Consulates 143
Emergency Telephone
  Numbers 143
Fishing guide 144
Gambling 144
Insurance 145
Irritating Insects 145
Marinas 145
Media 146
Nightlife 147
Photography 147
Police 147
Post 148

Public Holidays,
  Annual Events
  and Festivals 148
Safety 150
Taxes 152
Taxis 153
Telephones 153
Time and Dates 154
Tipping 154
Toilets 154
Tourist Offices 155
Tourism Enquiries 155
Water 156
Weights and
  Measures 156

Index 157

Feature Boxes

Hot Spots 10
Beaches 19
Shopping 22
Getting Around
  The Keys 42/43
A Short Walking
  Tour: Old Town,
  Key West 78/79
The Dry Tortugas 90/1
Salt Water Fishing
  Calendar for the
  Florida Keys 96/97

Introduction

The Florida Keys, often referred to as Florida's Caribbean Islands, are a chain of more than 800 tropical islands and islets, strung out like a delicate necklace in the turquoise water. Each of the Keys has a character and flavour of its own, and together they combine to offer one of the world's great tourist destinations.

Apart from the magnificent weather and miles of fabulous beaches, there are museums, theatres and historic places, world class fishing and diving, land and water-borne sports of all descriptions, a spectacular array of wildlife both on land and in the sea, great food and accommodation, and stunning sunsets.

Above all, the Keys have a style and pace of life that is unique, and that will draw you

back time and time again.

Any time of the year is a good time to visit the Keys. They are very busy from Christmas to May, but are fast becoming a year-round destination, attracting 3 million visitors annually.

The Keys have one of the world's largest charter fishing fleets, offer world-class diving, snorkelling and game fishing, and a wealth of wildlife, much of it rare. The beaches are a mecca for sunbathers, swimmers and sea shell collectors.

GEOGRAPHY

Florida covers an area of almost 58,665sq miles (152,066sq km) and acts as a barrier separating the Atlantic Ocean from the Gulf of Mexico. Its most northerly point is 100 miles (161km) south of the most southerly point in California, and the Keys are more than 1,500 miles (2,415km) further south than the French Riviera.

The Florida Keys are in Monroe County which covers an

area of 1,034 sq miles (2,680sq km), and takes in part of the **Everglades National Park** and the south-west corner of mainland Florida. The Keys themselves comprise more than 100 islands stretching south- westwards in a 126 mile (203km) sweep from the south-eastern tip of Florida.

The reefs off the Keys are the only living coral reef system in North America, and the third largest in the world. The word Key comes from the Spanish word 'cayo', which means a small island.

GETTING THERE

BY AIR

The main arrival airport is Miami which receives flights from all major international destinations. It is also the major hub for Central and South America. Most people arriving at Miami choose to pick up a rental car and drive down to the Keys, although Key West is only 45 minutes flying time from Miami, and rental cars are available at the island airport.

A number of major carriers, however, including American Eagle, ASA, Delta Connection, Continental Connection and US Air Express, operate regular, scheduled services into Key West and Marathon Airports. Many of these flights originate in Miami and connect with the international arrivals.

There are also a number of smaller airlines such as Cape Air from Naples and Fort Myers, Airways International and Gulf Stream International Airlines, which fly direct to the Keys from Miami and other cities in Florida and the Bah-amas. Car rentals are available at Marathon and Key West airports.

BY BUS

Greyhound Lines operates services to the Keys from Miami (☎ 800-410 Keys or ☎305 296 9072)

BY SEA

Cruise ships sail regularly to Key West and the waters around the Keys are very popular with yachts from around the world. The Intracoastal Waterway runs through Card and Barnes Sounds to Florida Bay, and is suitable for vessels with a draft of 5ft or less. Hawk Channel is the oceanside route, and a line of buoys marks the safe passage through the reefs and Keys.

Key West Express operates a ferry between Key West and Fort Myers Beach and Marco Island. ☎ 888-539-2628.

BY LAND

The only way to drive to the Keys is via the Florida mainland. From eastern Florida, US1 leads directly to the Keys, or you can take the Florida Turnpike.

After exit 49 on the Turnpike, watch out for the sign for **Homestead South**, which is the Turnpike Extension. It ends at Florida City where it connects with US 1 which leads to Key Largo. If visiting the northern end of Key Largo, you can take toll road 905A south, signed as **Coral Sound Road**, which crosses onto the island north of Crocodile Lake National Wildlife Refuge.

Through the Keys, US 1 is known as the **Overseas Highway** and it runs to Key West. If travelling south from Tampa along the Gulf coast, you have two choices. Take 1-75 south to Naples and then take Alligator Alley through the Everglades to the Miami exit, then go south to the Turnpike Extension. Or you can travel on US 41 South to Naples and then take the Turnpike Extension which runs southeast across the state to connect with US 1.

From Miami Airport, take Le-Jeune Road south to route 836 West to connect with the Turnpike Extension. Then drive south for US 1 and the Keys.

A BRIEF HISTORY

THE INDIANS

Many Indian tribes occupied different parts of Florida when the first European explorers arrived, with the fierce nomadic Calusas, allegedly 7ft (2m) tall, roaming through the Everglades and the Keys.

The Indians were fishermen, and they used the hardwood trees on the Keys to build their homes. It is thought that some Europeans, whose ships ran aground on reefs off the Keys, were held as slaves by the Indians, whose history and culture archaeologists are still trying to learn more about from their burial mounds. By 1750, however, imported diseases, slavery and war had wiped out almost all the Indians.

Florida was so-named by Juan Ponce de Leon, who sailed past the Keys and up the Atlantic Coast to land somewhere near present day St Augustine on Easter Monday, 15 May 1513. He thought he had discovered a new island in the Bahamas, and because of the luxuriant blossoms, he named it Florida after Pascua Florida, the traditional Spanish Feast of Flowers held during Easter.

Spanish chronicler Antonio de Herrera, who accompanied the expedition, wrote of the Keys: *'To all this line of islands and rock islets they gave the name of Los Martires (The Martyrs) because, seen from a distance, the rocks as they rose to view, appeared like men who were suffering; and the name remained fitting because of the*

Continued on p.12...

9

HOT SHOTS

KEY LARGO

Dolphins Plus Research Center
Learn more about these wonderful creatures at this educational facility.

John Pennekamp Coral Reef State Park
Fabulous snorkelling and scuba, glass-bottom boat tours, wildlife.

Key Largo Jules Undersea Lodge
The world's only underwater hotel, but non-guests are welcome in the marine park.

ISLAMORADA

Long Key State Park
Great beaches, wildlife, nature trails, canoeing and camping.

MARATHON

Crane Point Hammock
A dense woodland area rich in flora, fauna and history with archaeological sites.

Old Seven Mile Bridge
The world's longest fishing pier, great for birdwatching and enjoying the sea.

LOWER KEYS

National Key Deer Refuge
A wildlife sanctuary rich in bird, animal and plant life and home of the endangered Key deer.

KEY WEST

The Little White House
Built by President Harry S Truman for whenever he could escape Washington.

Mallory Square
Lively at most times but the place to be at sunset, both to watch the street entertainers and the sun go down.

Old Town
Fabulously atmospheric, historic area packed with things to see and do with shops, museums, attractions and great bars and eateries.

Above: The John Pennekamp Coral Reef State Park

Below: The Little White House, Key West

many that have been lost there since'. There is no record of any landing at that time on the Keys.

THE SPANISH

De Leon returned with another expedition in 1521 intending to establish a settlement on the mainland, but Indian attacks forced him to withdraw. The first Spanish settlement was established at St Augustine in 1565, making it the oldest European settlement anywhere in the US. The Spanish extended their control over the north of the state and later faced attack from both the English and French, but the Keys remained undeveloped.

THE ENGLISH

In the late eighteenth century the Keys became a haven for pirates and buccaneers, and in 1822 – 20 years before Florida became a state – the fledgling US Navy Pirate Fleet, a forerunner of the US Coastguard Service, founded a base on the islands to establish law and order, which in turn encouraged the first serious settlement.

The first settlers were farmers, many from the Bahamas, and groves of Key limes, tamarind and breadfruit were established. In the Lower Keys, pineapple farms initially thrived, and a large pineapple factory was built which provided canned pineapple to most of eastern North America.

These first English settlers became known as Conchs (pronounced 'konks'), partly because of the amount of these sea creatures that they ate, and also because they used the conch shells to signal to each other, especially when a ship was on the rocks.

In 1821 after Florida was ceded to the United States from Spain, these Bahamians were ordered to become US citizens or leave. Most chose to stay, and most moved their families to Key West. A true Conch is someone born on Key West, and the birth of a baby is still often announced by placing a conch shell on a stick in the front yard.

Later settlers looked to the sea for their living, and a shark factory thrived on Big Pine Key. It was built among the ruins of the abandoned farms. The sharks were skinned and the tough hide was salted down and sent to the home factory in New Jersey where it was processed into a tough leather called shagreen.

Other settlers on Key West and Islamorada earned their living as wreckers, salvaging goods from ships that went down on the nearby reefs. There are even stories that lights were deliberately set up on the reefs to lure the unsuspecting vessels on to the rocks. The prosperity of Key West was built on the profits of the wreckers. Over the last four centuries, at least 400 vessels have foundered in the treacherous waters off the Keys, making it one of the shipwreck capitals of the world.

Commercial fishermen and sponge divers were attracted to the islands, and then Cuban exiles brought their cigar-making skills, establishing factories on Key West. Until the early 1900s the only way of travelling between the Keys and to the mainland was by boat.

The railway

Tycoon Henry Flagler, who had made his fortune with John D. Rockefeller in Standard Oil, boosted the Keys' popularity with his 'impossible' railroad. The idea for the 'Railroad that crossed the sea' was born in 1905. It cost $27 million dollars to build and was a remarkable engineering feat. It also brought wealthy holidaymakers to the islands.

Flagler had already built a railroad down the eastern coast of Florida to Homestead, and in 1912, after years of hard work, the line was extended to Key West.

The Depression hit the Keys harder than almost anywhere else in the US. The city of Key West went bankrupt, and many people moved away.

It was then that Keys officials recognised that the islands did have something to offer — as a tropical holiday destination with sun, sea, sand and year-round good weather.

When the railroad was destroyed by a hurricane on Labor Day, 1935, plans for a highway connecting the islands were drawn up, and the Overseas Highway was opened in 1938, largely following the tracks of the railroad.

War

But the outbreak of World War II the following year, dashed any hopes for a tourist boom. During the war, the Navy built a pipeline which ran from Florida City to Key West and this was replaced in 1982, quadrupling the supply of water. All the islands' water is still piped in from the mainland.

The US Navy also came to the Keys' rescue by building a submarine base on Key West, and then shrimp, the Keys' 'pink' gold, were discovered.

Tourism

After the end of the war, tourism started to develop, and the 126-mile (203km) Overseas Highway was widened and modernised. Today, there are 42 scenic bridges connecting more than

Continued on p.16...

13

Above: Pier House, Key West
Below: Wave-runners, Plantation Key
Opposite: Cheeca Lodge, Islamorada

Inset: Sunset celebrations, Key West

100 islands in the Keys, the first being built at Jewfish Creek to join Key Largo to the mainland.

Tourism is the mainstay of the Keys' economy. Key Largo is known as the 'Diving Capital of the World', Islamorada is the 'Sport Fishing Capital', Marathon is the 'Heart of the Keys', and Key West is a wonderfully historic, eccentric city which is the haunt of artists and writers, museums and theatres, and much, much more.

WEATHER

The year-round good weather is the main reason people flock to the Florida Keys in their millions.

TEMPERATURE

There are two seasons — hot, humid and wet from June to September, and warm, mostly dry for the rest of the year. The average annual temperature on the Keys is 71°F (21°C), with Key West being warmest at an average annual temperature of 81.9°F (27°C).

January is the coolest month at about 70°F (21°C) and July the hottest at 84.5°F (29°C). Even during the hottest weather, there are usually welcome sea breezes which help cool one down a little, nature's own air-conditioning, and in the evening, the temperature drops to around 73°F (22.5°C), making it ideal for late-night moonlight strolls.

RAINFALL

Average annual rainfall is between 40 and 45 inches (102 and 114cm) a year. During the summer months there are often spectacular electrical storms and torrential downpours, usually accompanied by thunder and often in the late afternoon or early evening. These summer deluges rarely last for long, and can often be over in a few minutes.

If you are caught out in one of these downpours, especially if it is lightning, seek shelter at once. You normally get a little warning before it starts raining because the winds usually pick up and the temperature drops. As soon as the rain stops, however, both the temperature and humidity pick up again, and the rain water quickly evaporates.

If you are driving when it starts raining heavily, turn your headlights and windscreen wipers on, and reduce your speed. Exercise the greatest caution because the roads often flood, and there can be blinding spray and the danger of aquaplaning, especially if you have to brake quickly.

HURRICANES

There is a risk of hurricanes any time between June and November, with September the most at-risk month, but having said this, the risk of one actually hitting the islands is not great.

Hurricane Andrew, with winds of 164mph (264kph) which devastated Homestead, an area south of Miami in August, 1992, was the most severe storm to hit Florida for decades. Hurricane Wilma hit the Keys in October 2005. While there was severe flooding and some property damage, early warning and evacuation prevented any loss of life or serious injury. Within weeks almost all signs of the storm had been erased.

On average, a hurricane can be expected to hit Florida about once every 5 years, and the vast majority of these cause minimal damage. Florida can expect to be affected by an offshore hurricane about once every two years.

Apart from fierce high winds and towering seas, torrential and sustained rainfall is the major feature associated with tropical storms and hurricanes. Florida's wettest day was in September, 1950 during hurricane activity, when 38.5 inches (98cm) of rain fell during a 24 hour period close to Cedar Key on the Central Gulf Coast.

Because of the potential threat of hurricanes, there is a very sophisticated tracking and alert system, and all tropical storms are monitored and their position announced on local radio and television. If there is a serious threat, there are clearly marked evacuation routes from the islands to the mainland, but in the unlikely event of this happening, listen to the media for the latest instructions.

THE PEOPLE

The resident population of Florida is about 13 million, but every year around 42 million holidaymakers descend on the Sunshine State, the world's top tourist destination. The Keys are in Monroe County, which has a resident population of 80,950 and Key West is the County Seat with a city population of 28,000. Each year, about 3 million tourists visit the Keys.

FLORA AND FAUNA

PLANTS

More than half of Florida is covered by forests and more than 300 types of trees have been identified together with over 3,500 other plants. The hardwood forests of the north give way to the tropical forests and mangrove swamps of the south and the Keys, with oak, pine, cypress, palm and mangrove predominating. You will also find Caribbean imports such as mahogany, gumbo-limbo, palms and palmettos.

Continued on p.20...

17

East Martello Tower, Key West

The manchineel tree

Found on many beaches, the manchineel tree has a number of effective defensive mechanisms which can prove very painful. Trees vary from a few feet to more than 30 feet in height, and have widely spreading, deep forked boughs with small, dark green leaves and yellow stems, and fruit like small, green apples. If you examine the leaves carefully without touching them, you will notice a small pin-head sized raised dot at the junction of leaf and leaf stalk. The apple-like fruit is very poisonous, and sap from the tree causes very painful blisters. It is so toxic, that early Caribs are said to have dipped their arrow heads in it before hunting trips.

Sap is released if a leaf or branch is broken, and more so after rain. Avoid contact with the tree, do not sit under it or on a fallen branch, and do not eat the fruit. If you do get sap on your skin, run into the sea and wash it off as quickly as possible.

BEACHES

Key Largo:	Harry Harris Park, John Pennekamp Coral Reef State Park
Islamorada:	Long Key State Recreation Area
Marathon:	Sombrero Beach Park
Lower Keys:	Little Duck Key Park, Bahia Honda State Recreation Park
Key West:	Fort Zachary Taylor State Historic Park, Higgs Beach, Smathers Beach

TANNING SAFELY

The sun is very strong but sea breezes often disguise just how hot it is. If you are not used to the sun, take it carefully for the first two or three days, use a good sun screen with a factor of 15 or higher, apply it frequently, and do not sunbathe during the hottest parts of the day when the sun is highest in the sky.

Wear sunglasses and a sun hat. Sunglasses will protect you against the glare, especially strong on the beach, and sun hats will protect your head. Remember that continued exposure to strong sun can cause eye cataracts and eyelids are especially vulnerable to skin cancer.

Smathers Beach, Key West

19

There are also trees bearing a wide range of edible fruits and nuts, from mango, papaya, carambola, banana and key lime to coconut. You will see lots of references to 'hammocks' on the Keys. A hammock is thought to be derived from the Arawak word 'hamaca', meaning a jungle or dense mass of vegetation. It now means an area of raised woodland.

Animals

The area has a rich and diverse wildlife and many rare animals, such as the Key deer and Vaca Key raccoon, both of which are protected. About 420 species of bird (the State Bird is the mocking bird), 700 species of fish, 25 species of lizard, 35 species of turtle, 57 species of amphibian, and 160 species of freshwater fish have been recorded in the Everglades and the Keys.

It is thought that animals migrated to the Keys when it was still joined to the mainland. The plain over which they crossed is now submerged and forms the shallow Florida Bay, and many species now on the Keys are smaller than their mainland relatives because they have had to adjust to the smaller environment in which they live.

Squirrels, raccoons, armadillos, porcupine and opossums are all common.

There are alligators (gators), now protected by law, snakes, frogs, lizards and turtles. Species only found on the Keys include the Lower Keys cotton rat, the Cudjoe Key rice rat, Key Largo woodrat, Vaco Key raccoon and Key Largo cotton mouse. There are also the Keys mud turtle and Keys mole slink.

Snakes

There are several species of snake but these generally keep away from humans and live in the remotest parts of the Keys. Species include the Keys ribbon snake, Big Pine Key ringneck, and several related species of rat snake. The cottonmouth, coral and rattlesnake are poisonous.

The Key Deer

The Key deer is a small member of the white-tail deer family, and is rarely more than 26 inches (66cm) tall at the shoulder. The buck is larger than the doe and usually weighs between 60 and 90 lbs (27 to 40kg). By 1949 it was believed there were only thirty of the species surviving in the wild, but numbers are now up to about 300. Dogs, cars and tropical storms are their main threats to survival.

Insects

There are hundreds of species of insects from irritating mosquitoes and tiny black flies (no-see-'ems), to spiders and, very rarely, scorpions.

Marine creatures

The warm waterways sometimes play host to the gentle and delightful manatee which needs all the protection it can get, while bottlenose dolphin are plentiful and can be seen around the Keys in coastal waters.

Seashells

The Keys provide rich pickings if you are a seashell collector. Pink conch shells up to 8 inches (20cm) long are sometimes washed up on the beach; Triton's trumpets are rare but can measure up to 9 inches (22cm).

Common shells include frog-shells, distorsios, volutes, tulips, murex, cones, olives, marginellas, cowries, augers and the Florida horse conch, the State's official shell which can grow up to 24 inches (61cm) long. Crown conch can be found near mangrove swamps and sheltered bays, and the smallest of the crown conch, melongena corona, comes from the Lower Keys. There are more than 50 species of beautiful tree snails which grow up to two inches (5cm) long.

The Reefs

The coral reefs are one of the Keys' greatest attractions and one of the most vulnerable.

Since 1986, the non-profit group Reef Relief has been installing and maintaining buoys over the reefs to allow boats to tie up to them rather than drop anchors on the coral. So far, 119 mooring buoys have been installed over seven sites.

Birds

Graceful white egrets can be spotted everywhere, you can see ospreys sitting in their nests atop telephone poles, and most people take home memories of the fantastic aerial acrobatics of pelicans which plunge into the sea after fish.

FOOD AND DRINK

From Gulf shrimps to Key lime pie, there is a wide range of wonderful fresh foods to enjoy.

SEAFOOD

There is yellowtail and mutton snapper, grouper, tiny grunt, dolphin (the fish *mahi mahi*, not the mammal), spiny lobster, oysters, giant pink shrimp and delicious stone crab, all from local waters. Stone crab are 'harvested' by local fishermen, who often remove only one of the crab's large claws. The crabs, we are assured, are

SHOPPING

Most shops are open from 9am to 5pm Monday to Saturday, while stores in shopping malls often stay open until 10pm. In tourist areas, shopping hours are very flexible and some stores never close.

There is a huge range of goods to choose from to take home as souvenirs, from local arts and crafts to antiques, and from the latest fashions to interestingly shaped pieces of whitened driftwood.

Driftwood is often fashioned into works of art and offered for sale, together with coconut products and woven straw items, such as hats, baskets and wall hangings. Sea shells are used widely by local artists in their works. There are mobiles, hand-made jewelry, hand-made pottery and leather goods.

There are many shops selling fashions and fabrics designed and printed on the islands. The Keys are particularly known for antique shops and specialist book shops. And there are specialist Keys products such as Key West fragrances, and food items made from locally produced fruits, such as juices and jellies.

Duval Street, looking towards Sloppy Joe's Bar, Key West

then returned to the sea where another claw will grow within a few months.

Seafood can be eaten grilled, boiled, baked or sautéed. It is used to make delicious soups, chowders and stews, and lobster and crab are delicious cold and served with a mayonnaise sauce.

Conch (pronounced konk), are highly nutritious, and can be served in a variety of ways. They can be grilled, ground in conch burgers, fried in batter as fritters, or eaten raw in salads.

INTERNATIONAL CUISINE

Another culinary treat is the number of different ethnic cuisines available on the Keys,

Above: African Queen Jetty, Key Largo
Below: Clinton Square Market, Key West

from Cuban to Chinese, Caribbean to Italian and German to Japanese.

You can try Cuban-inspired 'lechon', which is roast pork flavoured with garlic and tart oranges grown on the Keys. The oranges get their tartness from the limestone soil and give the dish a unique flavour.

Other dishes include ropa vieja (old clothes), which is a beef dish, and picadillo, a hamburger-caper-raisin mixture served with a savoury sauce. All are usually served with boiled white or yellow rice, flavoured with either saffron or bihol, and black beans.

Puddings include 'flans', such as baked and caramelised custard and guava shells stuffed with cream cheese, to fresh tropical fruits perhaps served with tropical fruit-flavoured ice cream. And, of course, there is Key Lime Pie, made with condensed or evaporated milk and the juice and minced rind of the piquant Key limes.

SPORTS AND PASTIMES

The Keys are an ideal venue for an active holiday, especially for aquatic pursuits.

There are hundreds of boats available for charter, either bareboard or fully crewed.

Thousands of visitors choose to bring their own boats and there are public boat ramps at the following: Blackwater Sound MM110B, Indian Key Fill MM79B, Marathon MM54B, Marathon Yacht Club MM49B, Seven Mile Bridge (west end), Spanish Harbor, Shark Fill Key, Cudjoe Key, Stock Island Ramp MM7, Key West, at the end of A1A.

CANOEING

Canoe rentals are available in many locations, and offer an exciting way of seeing the real Keys. You can paddle down backwaters inaccessible in any other way, and commune with nature and the spectacular wildlife. There are hundreds of miles to be paddled around the islands and along designated trails in the State Parks.

Use an effective insect repellant and good sun screen when canoeing. Before setting out, check on the conditions likely to be encountered and decide whether you have the necessary skills to cope with them, and always be alert to tides, weather and wind changes.

DIVING

The Keys offer world-class diving and attract more than a million divers and snorkellers annually. It is also a great place to learn how to scuba and snorkel because of the warm, clear waters and top dive schools.

24

The Keys boast miles of coral reefs, a very rich marine life, and scores of wrecks waiting to be explored. Snorkelling skills can usually be acquired after about 15 minutes' of lessons, and all you need is a mask and snorkel for breathing, and flippers for propulsion.

Scuba diving requires training to learn technique and how to use the complicated equipment. Instruction by qualified teachers can lead to certification which entitles you to dive anywhere in the world. A four day course is usually adequate to certify for open water diving.

The **Florida Keys National Marine Sanctuary**, which includes the entire island chain from northernmost Key Largo south to the Dry Tortugas, was established in 1990. It is further evidence of the importance placed on conserving the offshore environment, which started with the establishment of the **John Pennekamp Coral Reef State Park** off Key Largo in 1960.

Off the Lower Keys, there is the **Looe Key National Marine Sanctuary**, which banned spearfishing and shell and coral collecting in 1981.

Molasses Reef claims to be the world's most popular dive site because of its easy access, clear, warm waters and stunning array of tropical fish.

There are scores of excellent dive sites, and some of the best are included in the FactFile at the back of the book.

Fishing

Fishing is almost a way of life in Florida, and especially in the Keys. People fish for both food and sport. Florida saltwater and freshwater fishing licenses are needed for all out of state anglers aged 16 and older. Florida residents do not need a licence if salt fishing from land or a pier. All fees collected are used specifically for improving and restoring fish habitats, building artificial reefs, researching marine life and habitats, enforcement and education.

Do not damage or take coral, disturb marine mammals, take turtle eggs, take or harvest conch, exceed catch limits, use spearguns within 300yds (91m) of public beaches and piers, or in prohibited areas.

Licences are obtained from county tax collector offices and local fishing and bait shops. Fishing charters and cruises are widely available throughout the area. It is often best to go in a group or be prepared to join one as this cuts the cost down. Most charters include the cost of boat, equipment, bait and guides.

GOLF

There is a 9-hole course at **Key Colony Beach** (☎ 289-1533), near Marathon, open to non-guests, and an 18-hole par-72 course at the **Key West Club** on Stock Island (☎ 294-5232) which is available at certain times to the playing public.

The **Marathon 18-hole Championship Course** is only open to other country club members who have club IDs.

TENNIS

There are plenty of opportunities for a game either at public courts or those run by the larger hotels and resorts. If you want to play tennis, book courts early in the morning or late in the afternoon for the first few days until you acclimatise to the sun, and remember to drink lots of fluids both during and after the game.

WATERSPORTS

There is probably a greater choice of watersports here than anywhere else, and there are hundreds of shops selling and renting equipment. Many hotels and motels offer free use of equipment or will rent it out, and there are opportunities to learn a wide range of water-sport activities from qualified instructors throughout the islands.

Yachting

The islands' calm, warm waters attract vessels from around the world, and there are many full service marinas throughout the Keys. Most accommodation offers docks and yacht slips if you want to spend a few days ashore, and there are thousands of craft available on short and long-term charters either with or without crew.

CLASSIFICATION OF THE KEYS

The Florida Keys are divided into three sections – the Upper, Middle and Lower Keys. The Upper Keys run from Key Largo to Long Key, the Middle Keys from Grassy Key to Bahia Honda Key, and the Lower Keys from Big Pine Key to Stock Key. Key West stands alone at the end of the chain.

The best way to tour them by road is to start at the Florida mainland, drive the length of the Overseas Highway to Key West and then return along the same route taking in everything you missed on the way down, and doing again all those things that you really enjoyed. Many of the outlying Keys are only accessible by boat.

KEY LARGO

The first 18 miles (29km) of US 1 from Florida City – known as the Eighteen Mile Stretch – cross Jewfish Creek (MM108) to the island of Key Largo, which means 'Long Island', although part of the town was originally known as Rock Harbor. It is 60 miles (96km) from Miami, and 30 miles (48km) long, making it the largest of the Keys.

The island achieved international fame after being used as the location for the steamy 1948 film *Key Largo*, which was directed by John Huston and starred Humphrey Bogart, Lauren Bacall and Edward G. Robinson. Today it attracts tourists, divers and fishermen.

Key Largo is known as the entrance to the Keys and the 'Diving Capital of the World', and attracts about 1 million divers and snorkellers a year. The sheer number of marinas, water-sports, dive shops, advertising signs and flags leave you in no doubt what is on offer. The red flags with a diagonal white stripe are the international dive sign.

The north of the island is serviced by State Road (SR) 905, also called Card Sound Road, which runs onto the island along a toll road which crosses to the north of Crocodile Lake National Wildlife Refuge. The toll is $1 for cars. It then runs north to the tip of Key Largo with Angelfish Key and Palo Alto Key beyond, and south, through the centre of the Key to connect with US 1.

The Overseas Highway runs on to Key Largo and crosses Lake Surprise to connect with SR 905 at MM 106.5. The **Key Largo** **Chamber of Commerce and Florida Keys Visitor Centre** is at MM 106, and is worth a visit because it offers a wealth of information and brochures about the Keys and can help with questions about accommodation and so on. ☎ 1-800-822-1088.

To the east of this junction is **Rattlesnake Key**, and just beyond on the mainland-bayside is **Blackwater Sound**. The Intra-coastal Highway runs along the western side of the Key. The Overseas Highway crosses the Marvin D. Adams Waterway at MM 103.5.

MARINE ATTRACTIONS

Key Largo Undersea Park

Key Largo Undersea Park (MM 103) also boasts the world's first underwater hotel, **Jules**

Key Largo Hammocks State Botanical Park

Just before State Road (SR) 905 joins US1, it passes the Key Largo Hammocks State Botanical Park, which is open daily from dawn to dusk and admission is free. The park, opened in 1982, has an interpretive trail through a tropical hardwood hammock, and numbers painted on boulders beside the path correspond with those on the free trail guide available at the entrance.

Trees to be seen include the poisonwood, a relative of poison ivy, and the Jamaica dogwood, also known as the 'fish fuddle' tree, because its leaves are toxic to fish when placed in water. Bundles of leaves used to be dropped into a waterway, and the fish collected when they floated to the surface.

You can also spot fiddlewood, cocoplum, humbo-limbo, lobtolly, velvetseed, mahogany, pigeon plum, snowberry, Bahama strongbark, wild coffee, bamboo and strangler fig.

Undersea Lodge, where up to six guests can literally spend a night 30 feet (9m) beneath the waves observing the marine life through large port holes. The accommodation with all amenities, including room service, is in a 50 by 20 foot (16 by 6m) steel structure anchored to the sea bed.

However, you don't have to stay at the Lodge to enjoy the wonders of the Key Largo Underwater Park, which offers safe snorkelling because it is within an enclosed lagoon.

The marine park is designed to replicate the ocean's natural ecology and environment while providing easy access and enjoyment to divers and snorkellers of all skill levels.

Conducted tours allow snorkellers and divers to explore the underwater lodge, the working undersea marine research laboratory, marine archaeology experiments, and abundant marine plant and animal life.

The **Marine Lab Undersea Habitat for Science and Technology** offers divers and snorkellers a rare chance to watch underwater research projects in progress. There is also the 'accretion project' in which marine artists use materials from the sea to create sculptures.

The **Scott Carpenter 'Man In the Sea' Program** offers hands on experience using high-tech diving systems and equipment, through courses lasting from five to 11 days. Divers learn how to pilot one-man submarines, perform undersea lab experiments and study marine biology and underwater archaeology techniques. The park is open daily from 9am to 3pm. Admission is free ☎ 451-2353.

The Shipwreck Museum

The Maritime Museum of the Florida Keys (MM 102.6), also known as the Shipwreck Museum, features treasures recovered from shipwreck sites around the world, including the only US display of the 1733 Spanish Treasure Fleet, and the Haskins Capitana Medallion, a 1.8oz (51g) 22-carat gold medallion covered in diamonds, the rarest and most valuable artifact recovered from the Spanish ships. Open: daily ☎ 451-6444.

The John Pennekamp Coral Reef State Park

The John Pennekamp Coral Reef State Park (MM 102.5) contains the largest living coral in continental United States and was the first underwater state park in the country. It was founded in 1960 and is named after a late Miami newspaper editor who championed local environmental protection.

It is accessed off US 1, and covers 53,000 undersea acres

(21,200 hectares), and 2,350 upland acres (940 hectares). It is famous for its spectacular reefs and the wealth of marine life they support. More than 55 species of coral and over 500 species of tropical fish have been recorded in this 21 mile (34km)-long underwater garden.

You can also spot twenty-seven beautiful species of Gorgonians, which are related to anemones. There is brain and star coral, as well as staghorn and deep purple moosehead, and the coral plays hosts to vast quantities of sea creatures.

There are nine dive sites in the park — White Bank Dry Rocks, French Reef, Molasses Reef, Carysfort Reef, the Elbow, Key Largo Dry Rocks, Grecian Rocks, Cannon Patch and Conch Reef which is just outside the park's boundary.

The freighter *Benwood* was torpedoed by a German submarine dur-ing World War II and was limping home, when it was in collision with another vessel and eventually sank off French Reef.

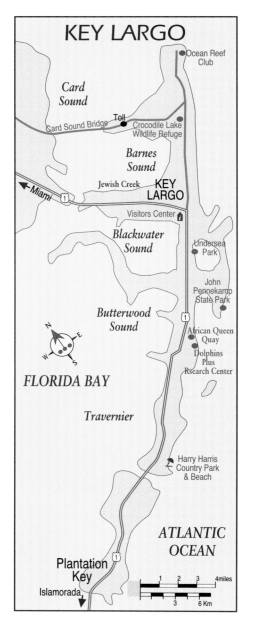

Above: Christ of the Deep, John Pennekamp Coral Reef, Key Largo
Below: The Marina del Mar, Key Largo

There is excellent snorkelling at White Bank Dry Rocks, and Molasses is the park's largest reef with a wide choice of underwater landscapes and marine life. Carysfort Reef is named after a British frigate, the *Carysford*, which ran aground in 1770, although why the reef is spelled differently is not clear. Cannon Patch gets its name because of the large number of cannon that have been found there.

The *San Jose*, a glass-bottom boat, makes the five mile trip out to Molasses Reef, the most popular reef on the park, three times a day for guided tours – at 9.15am, 12.15pm and 3pm. The *Scuba Express*, a 14 passenger boat, and the *Dive Express*, which carries 6 passengers, visit Molasses Reef, French Reef or Benwood Wreck, twice daily at 9.30am and 1.30pm. Trips include two hours of diving with two tanks at two locations. Participants must be experienced certified divers.

The *El Capitan*, *Sea Garden* and *Coral Sea* dive boats make three, two and a half hour trips daily, which allow 90 minutes for snorkelling. Most trips go to Grecian Rocks, which is so shallow that the coral sometimes breaks water at low tide. It is a great place for underwater photography because of the excellent visibility in the water, and the presence of colourful angelfish and parrotfish. There are also half day sailing and snorkelling trips aboard the *Lambada*, a 38ft (12m) catamaran.

The 510ft Spiegel Grove, a retired U.S. Navy Landing Ship Dock, is the largest ship ever intentionally sunk to create an artificial reef. It was sunk in 2002 and lies in 130ft of water

There is a tropical wood on the upland slopes (hammock) with the Wild Tamarind nature trail, and there is a boardwalk through the coastal mangrove swamps.

The park, which has 47 campsites, is very popular, and when it gets too busy it temporarily closes its gate. It has an excellent interpretive centre and also offers camping, picnicking, swimming, sea-fishing, ranger-guided hiking and canoe tours, snorkelling and scuba guided tours, diving and canoe rentals. There is a boat ramp and refreshments are available. Boat reservations ☎ 451-1621. Camping reservations ☎ 451-1202.

The **visitor centre** is open daily from 8am to 5pm and should be your first port of call. It offers a slide programme to familiarise you with the park, and also has aquariums and other exhibits. Reservations for the glass-bottomed boat trips are advisable ☎ 451-1621.

The Wild Tamarind nature trail starts close to the visitor

Key Largo National Marine Sanctuary

Key Largo National Marine Sanctuary (☎ 451-1644) is 3 miles (5km) offshore and a protected 100sq mile (161km) area of coral reef, seagrass and sand beds, offering spectacular diving. The Carysfort Lighthouse, built in 1852, is the oldest working lighthouse of its kind in the US.

The sanctuary contains several shipwrecks, and the 4,000lb (1,800kg) bronze statue 'Christ of the Deep', which stands in 25ft (8m) of water in Key Largo Dry Rocks in the Atlantic Ocean. It was installed as an underwater shrine, and stands on a 20 ton concrete block. Created by Italian sculptor Guido Galletti, it is a replica of the Christ of the Abysses which stands in 50ft (15m) of water off Italy. It was a gift to the Underwater Society of America from industrialist and undersea sportsman Egidi Cressi. It is one of the most photographed underwater sites in the world, and is a popular spot for underwater weddings.

Experienced scuba divers can explore the *Bibb* and *Duane*, two vintage Coast Guard cutters deliberately sunk off Key Largo in 1987 to create artificial reefs. They are just south of Molasses Reef. The 327ft (100m) vessels sit on white sand in 120ft (37m) of water. Experienced divers should still be accompanied by a Keys-based dive charter operator.

centre, and the mangrove trail starts further to the east. Rare migrating birds include mangrove cuckoos, black whiskered vireos and smooth billed anis.

Holiday Inn Key Largo Marina

The Holiday Inn Key Largo Marina, MM 100, has the original *African Queen* boat, skippered by Bogart in the film which also featured Katharine Hepburn. The vessel spends a lot of time touring the US on exhibition, but when it is docked, visitors can take a 45 to 60 minute ride ☎ 451-2121.

The marina continues the Hepburn link by featuring the *Thayer IV* which was used in the poignant movie *On Golden Pond*. The film starred Katharine Hepburn, Henry Fonda and daughter Jane Fonda. It was the last film made by Henry Fonda and won him an Oscar.

You can also visit the Caribbean Club MM 104, which was one of the locations for the Bogart-Bacall Key Largo movie.

The *Key Largo Princess* and *Coral Reef* Glass Bottom Boat (MM 100) ☎ 451-4655 both offer glass bottom boat tours to the reefs.

Dolphins Plus Research Center

At Dolphins Plus Research Center MM 100 ☎ 451-1993, there is the chance to swim

Above: See the dolphins at play at the Dolphin Research Center

Left: Exploring the creeks in the John Pennekamp Coral Reef State Park

Below: The Sheraton Key Largo Resort

with dolphins. There is a special marine orientation session which includes a 90-minute pre-swim seminar about the plight of endangered marine species. The center also offers extended group sessions, up to six days long, which focus on dolphins and their habits.

Much of the center's work concentrates on the therapeutic benefits that sick and handicapped people can gain from swimming with these creatures. Telephone for information about seminars and swimming with the dolphin sessions.

OTHER ATTRACTIONS

The **Port Largo airstrip** is just to the south-east of Newport. US1 then runs past Rodriquez Key to the east to the southern tip of Key Largo, and the turn off for **Harry Harris County Park** (MM 92.5), a popular beach area with playground, tidal pools and covered picnic areas with barbecue grills ☎ 852-7161.

Tavernier

Tavernier (MM 92) was first settled by farmers and fishermen from Key West in the 1860s. It is just to the south of the island's original settlement which was called Planter.

Tavernier itself gets its name from a small offshore key, which the early Spanish called Tabona Key because of the horsefly.

Tavernier was badly hit by the 1935 hurricane and most of the buildings were destroyed. These were replaced by four-room Red Cross homes built of reinforced concrete and steel, designed to withstand future hurricanes. Unfortunately salt water was used to mix the concrete and eroded the steel, but you can still see some of these homes today.

The arrival of the railroad saw a period of rapid growth with many fruit farms being established. Many old frame buildings have already been restored as part of the long-term project to revitalise the historic district, and there is the old Methodist Church.

Florida Keys Wild Bird Rehabilitation Center

Since it opened in 1991, the centre has rescued and rehabilitated hundreds of birds, and you can see pelicans, spoonbills, hawks, owls, ospreys and other species which are currently patients. The centre's full-time staff are supported by volunteers. There are also conducted tours of the centre. Admission is free but donations are welcomed. Open daily (MM 93) ☎ 852-4486.

Just south of town at MM91 is a shopping centre and the road then crosses over Tavernier Creek which separates Key Largo and Plantation Key.

Continued on page 39...

EATING OUT ON KEY LARGO

Anthony's $$-$$$
Fine Italian dining
97630 Overseas Highway
☎ 853-1177
Open for dinner.

Bogie's Cafe, Holiday Inn $-$$
Seafood and steak
☎ 451-2121
Open all day.

Cheng Garden $-$$
Chinese
101443 Overseas Highway
☎ 453-0600
Open from lunch to dinner.

Coconuts (MM 100) $-$$
Fine seafood and steaks
Marina del Mar
☎ 453-9794
Open for lunch and dinner.

Copper Kettle (MM 91.8) $
American
Tavernier
☎ 852-4113
Open from breakfast to lunch.

Country Gulls (MM 90) $
Island home cooking
Tavernier Towne Shopping Center
☎ 852-8244
Open from lunch to dinner.

Cracked Conch $
Seafood
105045 Overseas Highway
☎ 451-0732
Open from lunch to dinner, closed Wednesday.

Craig's Restaurant (MM 90.5) $-$$
Seafood and American
Tavernier
☎ 852-9424
Open from early lunch to dinner.

Denny's Latin Cafe (MM 100) $
Cuban
☎ 431-3665
Open 24 hours.

Flamingo $-$$
American
Garden Cove Drive
☎ 451-8022
Open from lunch to dinner.

Fish House Restaurant and
Seafood Market (MM 102.4) $$
Great seafood and steaks
☎ 451-4665
Open daily.

Ganim's Kountry Kitchen
(MM 100) $
American home cooking
☎ 451-3337
Open breakfast to lunch.

Great Wall (MM 91) $
Chinese
Tavernier Towne Shopping Center
☎ 852-8508
Open from lunch to dinner.

Gus' Grille $
American
103800 Overseas Highway
Key Largo
☎ 453-0000
Open for lunch and dinner.

Inexpensive $ Moderate $$ Expensive $$$

Harriette's (MM 95.5) $
Great home cooking
☎ 852-8689
Open from early breakfast to lunch.

Hideout Restaurant (MM 103.5) $
American
☎ 451-0128
Open for breakfast and lunch.

Howard Johnson Restaurant
(MM102.3) $-$$
American
☎ 451-2032
Open all day.

Marlin Restaurant $-$$
Seafood
102770 Overseas Highway
☎ 451-9555
Open nightly for dinner.

Old Tavernier Restaurant
(MM 90.5) $$
Italian
☎ 852-6012
Open for dinner.

Pilot House Marina Restaurant $$
Seafood and American
North Channel Drive
☎ 451-3452
Open from early lunch to dinner.

Port Largo Coffee Shop (MM 100) $
Home cooking,
☎ 451-2999
Open from early breakfast to lunch.

Quay Restaurant (MM 102) $$
Mesquite grill, try alligator dishes
☎ 451-0943
Open from early dinner.

Senor Frijoles (MM 103.9)
$-$$
Latin American
Key Largo
☎ 451-1592
Open for dinner.

Snappers (MM 94.5) $-$$
Seafood and steaks
Seaside Avenue
☎ 852-5956
Open from early lunch to dinner.

Snook's Bayside $$-$$$
Award winning food
Key Largo
☎ 453-3799
Open for lunch and dinner.

Sundowners (MM 104) $-$$
Seafood and American
☎ 451-4502
Open daily 11am to 10pm.

Treetops (MM 97) $$
West Indian-Floridian
Sheraton Resort
☎ 852-5553
Open for dinner.

Tropical Cafe (MM 90.5) $-$$
Seafood and fine American
☎ 852-3251
Open from early breakfast to lunch.

The Keys are great fun for kids. This is at Islamorada

NIGHTLIFE

Caribbean Club (MM 104) ☎ 451-9970. Part of the film *Key Largo* was shot in the club which is open 24 hours a day.

Coconuts (MM 100) ☎ 453-9795. Very lively nightspot featuring disco and bands.

ISLAMORADA OR THE PURPLE ISLES

This is the name given to the group of islands comprising Plantation Key, Windley Key, Upper Matecumbe Key, Lower Matecumbe Key and Long Key.

They are noted for their beauty, the surrounding coral reefs and their excellent fishing for sailfish, backfin, tuna, cobia, dolphin, blue marlin, bonefish, tarpon, king mackerel, white marlin, swordfish, grouper, mutton, snapper and yellowtail.

There are fishing competitions and tournaments throughout the year, many attracting world-class fishermen. Islamorada is pronounced 'Eye-lam-or-a-dar'.

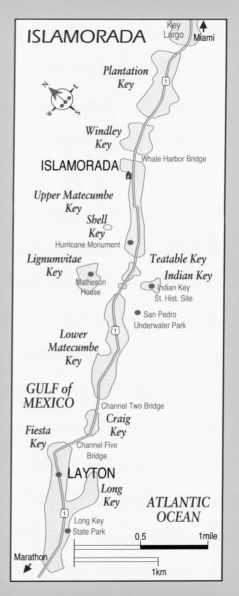

39

The Purple Isles Art Group sponsors exhibitions through the islands during the year.

PLANTATION KEY

Plantation Key has a resident population of about 6,830, and many fine shops and galleries to visit at **Treasure Village** (MM 86.7). ☎ 852-0511

Arts and Crafts

The village, which looks like a castle set among palm trees and lush vegetation, has galleries which include **Art Lovers**, which offers work by local artists, glass etchings, sculpture and limited edition prints. Open daily 10am to 6pm ☎ 664-3675.

Birds of Paradise specialises in tropical birds and fish sculpted in wood, ceramic, fibreglass and many other materials. Open daily 10am to 6pm ☎ 852-7255.

You can watch the potters at work at the **Bluewaters Potters' Gallery** and even have a go yourself. Open daily 10am to 6pm ☎ 853-0616.

The **Grant Gallery** offers island landscapes, seascapes and natural history paintings by local artists, open daily 11am to 6pm ☎ 664-2030.

Ichiban Custom Frames also has on-site potters and artists at work, open 10.30am to 5pm ☎ 852-1624.

Shipwreck treasures can be bought at **Somewhere in Time**

Windley Key

This popular resort key (MM 85) is now named after an early settler, although it was originally two Keys and known as Umbrella Keys, because its shape resembled an inverted umbrella. The two keys are now connected by a land bridge. Shortly after driving onto the key you pass Tropical Reef Resort.

In 1908 the island was purchased by the Florida East Coast Railroad because of its limestone deposits which were quarried to provide a bed for the track and embankments. These excavations are now the Windley Key Fossil Reef State Geological Site (MM 85) and attract geologists, students and fossil hunters interested in the incredible fossilized coral structures which have been exposed, and which are protected. The site is open for guided tours from 8am to 2pm every third Saturday of the month ☎ 664-2540.

The Theater of the Sea (MM 84.5) is in another former

Again, as well as scrimshaw and jewelry, open daily 10am to 6pm ☎ 664-9699. The **Tavernier Bronze Foundry** produces wonderful bronze works by local and Floridian

quarry site on the oceanside of the island. The facility opened in the late 1940s. It offers the chance to see a wide variety of marine life and interact with it, and the opportunity ($75 per person: three sessions a day) to swim with the dolphins if you reserve well in advance. There are also 'bottomless' boat rides, and shows featuring bottlenose dolphin, sea lions, sharks and other marine species throughout the day in the coral grotto. Open daily 9.30am to 4pm ☎ 664-2431.

Windley Key and Upper Matecumbe Key are separated by Whale Harbor (☎ 664-4511); the area teems with marinas and charter fishing boats, especially those with their high towers known as tuna towers.

The huge Holiday Isle resort and marina (MM 84), a complex that includes four hotels, dominates the end of the island. It hosts a wide range of sports and cultural events during the day, and it is a very lively place by night.

artists, open daily 10am to 6pm ☎ 852-8935.

The **Rain Barrel** (MM 86.5) is a community of artists that offers the chance to watch local artists and craftsmen at work and buy paintings, woodcarvings, hand-made jewelry and weaving. It also incorporates the Joan Purcell **Sunshine Art Gallery** (☎ 852-3960). Both the Rain Barrel (MM 86.5) and **Treasure Village** (MM 86) host a number of arts and crafts shows during the year, and offer the opportunity for shopping.

The Coast Guard Station (MM 86) is by Snake Creek, before the bridge across to Windley Key.

The **Redbone Gallery** at MM81.5, specialises in seascape paintings and sculptures. It is open daily 10am to 5.30pm ☎ 664-2002.

You can also visit **Bahama Bob's Flotsam and Jetsam** (MM 86), **Stacie Krupa Studio Gallery of Art**, 83 Oceanside and **The Gallery** at Morada Bay (MM81.6)

UPPER AND LOWER MATECUMBE KEYS

The islands get their name from the Indians' habit of enslaving any sailors washed ashore after being shipwrecked on the nearby reefs. The name comes from the Spanish words 'matar' (to kill) and 'hombre' (man).

Islamorada

Islamorada is on Upper Matecumbe Key, the main island of the Purple Isles. It has a resident population of 8,285 and is the home of the Key's largest charter

Continued on page 44...

GETTING AROUND THE FLORIDA KEYS

The Overseas Highway or US 1 is the only route through the Keys. It follows the path of the Overseas Railroad, and crosses 43 bridges on its 113 mile (182km) island leap-frogging route from leaving the Florida mainland coast to Key West. In 1982, thirty-seven bridges were replaced with wider, heavier spans, including Seven Mile Bridge at Marathon. Although it is an interstate highway, for most of its route in the Keys it is only a two-lane highway. It offers staggering scenery, passing emerald-green lagoons, turquoise seas, gently waving palms and olive-green mangroves. You may see dolphins offshore and herons, pelicans, spoonbills and ospreys. The journey between Miami and Key West can be travelled in less than four hours, but the whole idea of visiting the Keys is to slow down, so what's the hurry?

As it is a very long continuous road, properties along its route have huge house numbers in their addresses: ie Gilbert's Motel on Key Largo is 107900 Overseas Highway.

Mile Markers (MM) are positioned every mile along the Overseas Highway so that you always know where you are. They indicate the distance between Florida City and Key West. As you leave Florida City the marker bears the number 126, and when you get to the end of the road at the corner of Fleming and Whitehead Streets on Key West, the marker has the number 0. The 113 miles (182km) stretch of road over water and the Keys crosses forty-three bridges (one an overpass on land) which together account for almost 19 miles (30km) of the route.

Mile Markers are quoted throughout this guide and on maps, as they are almost universally used to identify the location of restaurants, hotels and attractions, and if you ask directions from a resident, you are likely to be told to look out for a particular mile marker number. As a general guide Key Largo falls between mile markers 110-87, Islamorada between mile markers 86 and 66, Marathon between mile markers 65 and 40, Big Pine Key and the Lower Keys between mile markers 39 and 9, and Key West between mile markers 8 and 0.

Greyhound buses operate services between Miami and Key West, with various stops along the way.

The bridges as you meet them from the mainland are:

Jewfish Draw Bridge at MM 106
223 ft (68m)
Key Largo Cut at MM 103.5
360 ft (110m)
Tavernier Creek at MM 91
320 ft (98m)
Snake Creek at MM 86
230 ft (70m)
Whale Harbor at MM 84
270 ft (82m)
Tea Table Relief at MM 80
270 ft (82m)
Tea Table at MM 79
700 ft (213m)
Indian Key at MM 78
2,460 ft (750m)
Lignumvitae at MM 77.8
860 ft (262m)
Channel 2 at MM 73
1,760 ft (537m)
Channel 5 at MM 71
4,580 ft (1396m)
Long Key MM 65
12,040 ft (3670m)
Tom's Harbor 3 at MM 61
1,270 ft (387m)
Tom's Harbor 4 at MM 60
1,460 ft (445m)
Vaca Cut at MM 53
300 ft (91m)
Seven Mile at MM 47
35,830 ft (10,924m)
Little Duck Missouri at MM 39
840 ft (256m)
Missouri-Ohio at MM 39
1,440 ft (439m)
Ohio-Bahia Honda at MM 38
1,050 ft (320m)
Bahia-Honda at MM 36
6,734 ft (2053m)
Spanish Harbor at MM 33.5
3,380 ft (1030m)

North Pine at MM 29.5
660 ft (201m)
South Pine at MM 28.5
850 ft (259m)
Torch Key Viaduct at MM 28
880 ft (268m)
Torch-Ramrod at MM 27.5
720 ft (220m)
Nile Channel at MM 26
4,490 ft (1369m)
Kemp's Channel at MM 23.5
1,030 ft (314m)
Bow Channel at MM 20
1,340 ft (409m)
Park at MM 18.5
880 ft (268m)
North Harris at MM 18
430 ft (131m)
Harris Gap at MM 17.5
140 ft (43m)
Harris at MM 16
430 ft (131m)
Lower Sugar Load at MM 15.5
1,260 ft (384m)
Saddle Bunch 2 at MM 14.5
660 ft (201m)
Saddle Bunch 3 at MM 14
760 ft (232m)
Saddle Bunch 4 at MM 13
900 ft (274m)
Saddle Bunch 5 at MM 12.5
900 ft (274m)
Shark Channel at MM 11.8
2,090 ft (637m)
Rockland Channel at MM 10
1,280 ft (390m)
Boca Chica at MM 6
2,730 ft (832m)
Stock Island at MM 5
360 ft (110m)
Key West at MM4
159 ft (48m)

fishing fleet, and is the sport-fishing capital of the world. The charter fleet includes both deep-sea boats and shallow water 'backcountry' boats.

There are a number of suggestions of how it came by its name. It is said that early Spanish sailors named it 'islas moradas' after the purple shells of sea snails they found on the beaches. It has also been suggested that the name comes from a small wild flower found all over the island. Less exciting is that the name comes from a Spanish dialect word which simply means 'homestead'. There is evidence, however, that Indians settled on the island hundreds of years ago.

Whatever the origin of its name, Islamorada is an elegant area with impressive resorts, lots of sporting amenities, and great diving and sea fishing. It created one of the first nature walks in the Keys, and was one of the first to produce a cycle path.

The US Post Office is at MM 83, ☎ 664-4738. People wanting to cool off after visiting the town library, can have a dip behind the building in the stream which runs through a grove of mangroves. There is a small man-made beach and picnic tables.

The **Fish Bowl** bowling alley is at MM 83.5. ☎ 664-9357.

The island, which was an important farming area at the beginning of the twentieth cen-tury, quickly developed into a world class fishing resort, first with the arrival of the railroad, and even more so, after the open-ing of the Overseas Highway.

The Islamorada Chamber of Commerce is in the heart of Islamorada's business district, and you cannot miss it as it is housed in a bright red railroad carriage at MM 83 ☎ 664-4503.

The **Hurricane Monument** (MM 81.5) ☎ 664-4645, marks the mass graves of those who perished when a hurricane hit with devastating force on 2 Sep-tember – Labor Day, 1935. Winds of 200mph (322kph) were recorded and more than 420 people were killed. Hun-dreds more were killed when an evacuation train carrying rail-road workers, most of them World War I veterans, was blown off the tracks and swamped by an 18ft (5.5m) high tidal wave. Huge sections of the Flagler rail-road were destroyed. A stone angel on a grave at Islamorada was one of the few things that survived the hurricane. It now stands in the Pioneer Cemetery in the grounds of Cheeca Lodge (MM 82) minus one hand and part of a wing.

Other attractions

Tarpon Flats (MM 81.1) is on the bay and has attracted many of the world's top anglers. The offshore waters are famous for tarpon and

LIGNUMVITAE KEY STATE BOTANICAL SITE

(MM 78.5)

The site is half a mile (0.8km) off the northwestern tip of Lower Matecumbe and only accessible by boat. A visit is highly recommended to get some insight into how the Keys must have looked before the developers arrived.

Scientists claim that some of the island vegetation is more than 10,000 years old. The island is special because of its virgin tropical hardwood hammock (wooded slope), similar to those found in the West Indies. Trees include lignumvitae, gumbo limbo, mangrove, mastic, poisonwood, pigeon plum, button-wood, strangler fig, mahogany and other unusual species. To date more than 130 tree species have been identified.

Early Spanish explorers thought the very heavy and hard lignumvitae wood (meaning wood of life) had special properties, and huge areas were felled and shipped back to Spain.

The term 'hammock' is slightly misleading, as the highest point on the island is only 18ft (5.5m) above sea level, and this is the highest point in the Keys until Key West. The 280 acre (112 hectare) stand of tropical vegetation is popular with butterflies and attracts many species, and there are at least 58 different species of versatile and large tree snail. Interesting birds that can be seen include mangrove cuckoos, black-whiskered vireos, smooth-billed anis, brown pelicans, ospreys, white-crowned pigeons, double-crested cormorants, gulls, terns, waders and many species of migratory warblers.

The island was bought by Miami financier William Matheson in 1919, who built a four-bedroom house from coral rock. The garden was planted with the help of botanist David Fairchild, and cannon from the *HMS Winchester*, which sank on Carysfort Reef in 1695, decorated the grounds. A boat dock and huge cistern was built to hold water, and power of a sort was supplied by a windmill.

Trails were created, an air strip built and all sorts of exotic animals such as Angora goats, Galapagos tortoises and Indian geese were introduced. The family owned the island until 1953.

The State of Florida acquired the Key in 1972 and declared it a protected state botanical site. The imported animals that had not died were removed, and the island has now reverted to its former state. There is an interpretive centre and visitor centre in the former Matheson house. There are ranger-led hiking and guided tours, and boats for the island leave from Indian Key Fill at MM 79.5 on US1.

Access to the island by private boats is limited, but they can dock at the island jetty and join ranger led tours between Thursday and Monday at 10.30am, 1pm and 2.30pm. There is a small tour charge. Only 50 people are allowed on the Key at any one time. Walking shoes and mosquito repellent are strongly recommended (☎ 664-4815).

Theater of the Sea, Windley Key

sailfish catches, and former President George Bush is one of the many keen fishermen who regularly return to these waters.

Offshore you can explore the **Coral Underwater Sea Garden** using scuba or snorkelling gear, and dive down to the *Eagle*, a 287 ft (88m) freighter sunk in 1985 by the Florida Keys Artificial Reef Association in an area devoid of reefs.

The Islamorada-based **National Center for Shipwreck Research** (☎ 852-1690) has, for the last five summers, been introducing divers to the thrills of treasure-seeking as part of the *Dive Into History* programme. Instead of bringing back treasure, however, the divers take photographs, collect archaeological data and learn the skills of underwater mapping. Courses last from two to ten days and lead to certification as an archaeological research diver.

If you fancy a game of tennis, the **Islamorada Tennis Club** at MM81 (☎ 664-5340) welcomes non-members.

At MM 79.9 you can visit the small but interesting **International Fishing Museum** (☎ 664-2767), next to the marina. It displays the area's fishing history, old angling equipment and encourages people to record their catches on photographs and then release them, in the interests of conservation. It is open daily.

INDIAN KEY

Indian Key Historic State Park (MM 78.5) is off Teatable Key and only accessible by boat. There is an observation tower overlooking the 12-acre (5 hectares) island. The island was named 'Mantanzas' by the Spanish, after their word for massacre. According to legend, 400 French shipwrecked sailors were slaughtered by the Caloosa Indians as they struggled ashore.

The island later became the site of a wreckers' camp and a thriving port in the 1830s. There used to be warehouses, wharves, store and a hotel. The salvage operation under the control of John Jacob Housman, was so profitable that Indian Key was the county seat of Dade County until it was destroyed in 1840, during an attack by Seminole Indians outraged at the takeover of their territory.

Sixteen of the settlement's 55 inhabitants were killed, the island was abandoned and the county seat moved to Miami on the mainland. There are three-hour guided tours of Indian Key which leave from Indian Key Fill on US1. Phone to check departure times ☎ 664-4815.

The battle between the Indians and the settlers is re-enacted every year during October as part of the **Indian Key Festival**.

Right: The Keys Visitor Center, Key Largo

Below: Port Antigua, Islamorada

Just south of Indian Key is San Pedro Underwater Archaeological Park, the site of the wreck of a 1733 Spanish treasure galleon.

EATING OUT ON ISLAMORADA

Atlantic's Edge (MM 82) $$-$$$
Fine American, excellent seafood
and attractive wine list
Cheeca Lodge Hotel
☎ 664-4651
Open for dinner.

Bentley's (MM 82.5) $-$$
Seafood and steaks
☎ 664-9094
Open for dinner.

Coral Grill (MM 83.5) $-$$
American
☎ 664-4803
Open for dinner nightly and
Sunday buffet lunch.

Fisherman's Kettle (MM 80.9) $
Seafood and steaks
☎ 664-4887
Open for lunch and dinner.

Green Turtle Inn (MM 81.5) $$
Seafood and steak
☎ 664-9031
Open from lunch to dinner,
closed Monday.

Grove Park $
Great ice cream parlour.

Horizon Restaurant (MM 84)
$$-$$$
Seafood and International,
Holiday Isle Resort
☎ 664-2321
Open all day, very fine dining.
Reservations recommended.

Howard Johnson Restaurant
(MM 84) $-$$
American, ☎ 664-9781
Open all day.

Jaws Raw Bar (MM 84) $
Seafood and snacks
Holiday Isle
☎ 664-2321
Open from 11am to 10pm.

Little Italy Restaurant
(MM 68.5) $
Italian
Long Key, ☎ 664-4472
Open for breakfast, lunch and
dinner.

Lorelei Restaurant (MM 82) $$
Seafood and steaks, lively
atmosphere, great food
Islamorada Yacht Basin
☎ 664-4656
Cabana Bar for breakfast and
lunch, restaurant for dinner, live
music nightly.

Lovin' Dough (MM 81) $
Fresh baked items
Bayside restaurant and bakery
☎ 664-2310
Open from breakfast
to lunch.

Manny and Isa's Kitchen
(MM 81.6) $
Spanish, Cuban and American
☎ 664-5019
Open from lunch to dinner,
closed Tuesday.

Marker 88 (MM 88) $-$$
International
Plantation Key
☎ 852-9315
A very popular water-front restaurant which offers fine dining with touches of Caribbean, and great wines. Open for dinner. Closed Monday. Reservations recommended.

Mexican Cantina (MM 81.5) $
Mexican
☎ 664-3721
Open lunch to dinner, closed Tuesday.

Ocean Terrace $$
Seafood and grill
Cheeca Lodge
☎ 664-4651.

Plantation Yacht Harbor
(MM 87) $$
Seafood and continental
☎ 852-2381
Open daily.

Rum Runners Island
Bar and Deli (MM 84) $
Seafood, salad and snacks
☎ 664-2321
Open 10am to midnight.

Scooter's Pizza (MM 92.5) $-$$
Italian
☎ 852-9272
Open for dinner, closed Wednesday.

Smuggler's Cove
(MM 85.5) $-$$
Seafood and steaks
☎ 664-5564
Open all day.

Squid Row (MM 82) $-$$
Seafood and snacks
☎ 664-9865
Open for lunch and dinner.

Whale Harbor Inn (MM 83.5)
$-$$
Seafood
☎ 664-4959
Open for lunch and dinner,and noted for its weekend seafood buffets. Nightly entertainment in the Harbor Bar.

Woody's Italian Gardens
(MM 82) $$
Italian
☎ 664-4335
Open weekdays for lunch and nightly for dinner.

Ziggie's Conch Restaurant
(MM 83) $$
Seafood
Great food, especially conch, lobster and oysters and many daily specials are not on the menu.
☎ 664-3391
Open dinner, closed Thursday

The hurricane was responsible for sinking more than a score of Spanish galleons along the Keys. This wreck was discovered in the 1960s and although little remains of the vessel today, it is still a very popular site with divers, and coins and other artifacts are still discovered.

Seven concrete cannon and an eighteenth-century anchor have been placed around the site to add a few extra touches to the underwater nature and snorkelling trail. The cannon are replicas of those found on a sister ship in the New Spanish Fleet, and the project was under the guidance of an underwater archaeologist. The wreck lies in 18ft (5.5m) of water (☎ 664-4815).

Caloosa Cove (MM 73) close to Channel Two Bridge, is one of the world's best tarpon fishing areas. **Channel Two Bridge** leads from Caloosa Cove to Craig Key, and then Channel Five connects the Overseas Highway with Fiesta Key and Long Key.

LONG KEY

Layton was incorporated as a city in 1963 and covers 120 acres (48m) on the southern shores of Long Key.

Long Key State Recreation Park (MM 67.5) has a number of nature trails through the wooded hills which give an impression of how the islands must have looked a century or two ago. There are camping and picnic sites along the long, sandy beach. It is also a good area for exploring by canoe, and there is swimming and seafishing, and guided walks and camp fire programmes. There is an observation tower offering commanding views (☎ 664-4815). Close to MM 66 there is the short Layton Nature Trail. The looped trail takes you to the bay and back through a wide variety of Keys' woodland vegetation. Also close to MM 66 is a marker commemorating the site of the Long Key Fishing Club, which was founded in 1906 by Flagler. Its most famous president was author Zane Grey who was killed in the 1935 hurricane.

The Overseas Highway then crosses Long Key Bridge, the second longest in the Keys spanning 2.3 miles (3.7km), which connects Long Key and Conch Key, the first of the 'Marathon Keys'.

NIGHTLIFE

Tiki Bar, Kokomo Beach Bar and Horizon Restaurant at the Holiday Isles Resort, Plantation Yacht Harbor and the Dockside Bar (MM 83.5).

MIDDLE KEYS

The Middle Keys run from Conch Key to Pigeon and are separated from the rest of the islands by the two longest bridges along the Overseas Highway, the 2.3-mile (3.7km) Long Bridge Key to the north and east and the famous Seven Mile Bridge (11km) to the west.

Conch Key (MM 63) is very scenic with its small white fishermen's cottages huddled together round the small but bustling harbour. The highway then passes **Duck Key** (MM 61) which lies to the left, a 65-acre (25.6 hectares) gem of an island in the Atlantic Ocean. The island used to have shallow pools where seawater was evaporated so that the salt residue could be gathered, but the island was abandoned in 1937 when the

Grassy Key

Grassy Key is best known for the Dolphin Research Center (MM 59) at Marathon Shores (☎ 289-1121). It has guided tours about the work of the center, a non-profit teaching and research facility which liaises with universities and research groups around the world. The center started out in the 1950s as the Flipper's Sea School, and was where the original Flipper films were made.

Today, many 'burnt out' dolphins from attractions spend their 'retirement' at the center. There is also a turtle hospital. There are two chances daily between Wednesday and Sunday — at 9.30am and 1.30pm — to swim with the dolphins. You have to pay for the privilege ($90) but it is worth it to swim with these fabulous, intelligent creatures and early reservations are recommended. Mandy Rodriguez, Center Director, says the dolphins really enjoy their contact with people. The Center is open from Wednesday to Sunday, with educational walking tours at 11am, 12.30pm, 2pm and 3.30pm. Admission charge.

Grassy Key has several camp-grounds, trailer parks and fishing camps.

owner died, and it was not until 1955 that a causeway was built connecting it with the Overseas Highway, allowing careful development.

There was a railroad camp on **Knight Key** (MM 57) and at one stage neighbouring Pigeon Key housed almost 5,000 workers. When they got their wages, they would cross over to Boot Key (MM 48) where shops had sprung up to supply the men.

Crawl Key (MM 56) gets its name from the crawls or corrals, which were used to hold the sea turtles before they finished up as turtle soup and steaks. It is not certain if the name comes from the Spanish 'corral' or the Dutch 'kraal', but the crawls were made of rocks and driftwood, and could hold scores of these creatures.

The highway then passes **Little Crawl Key** on the oceanside, to **Long Point Key** (MM 56). At MM 55 there is a causeway to oceanside **Coco-plum Beach**. The residential development has an exotic name but coco-plums could never have been grown there as the soil is not rich enough.

Fat Deer Key is at MM 54, and the home of **Key Colony Beach**. The incorporated city connected by a causeway to US 1 has grown dramatically in the last few years and has a large number of private homes and condos available for rent. Many are by the sea or on canals which lead to the ocean. The island originally consisted largely of mangrove swamps, but the city with its residential and business areas now covers 284 acres (114 hectares), and offers a complete range of facilities including golf course and busy marina.

Key Colony Beach Golf Course at MM 53.5 (☎ 289-1533) is a 9-hole par 3 course open to the public, and the **Sombrero Country Club** at MM 50 (☎ 743-2551) has an 18-hole course which welcomes non-members. There is the popular Sombrero Public Beach (MM 50), and West Side Cinema if you want to take in a movie.

Vaca Key and the town of **Marathon** is the 'Heart of the Keys' and a mecca for fisher-men, divers, bird watchers, walkers and those who simply want to laze in the sun at one of the many luxury resorts. There is confusion about how the island got its name and there are two likely origins. One is that the Spanish named the island after the many manatees, or sea cows, in the area, and the other is that they named it after graz-ing cattle. As it is unlikely there was any ranching at that time, the former seems more prob-able.

In 1818 fishermen from Mystic in Connecticut set up a base on the island. By the middle of the nineteenth century, settlers arrived to start plantations growing tropical fruits and vegetables.

Marathon

You pass Marathon Airport, the only one on the Keys between Miami and Key West, and then arrive in Marathon, a 12,600 strong resident community.

It is one of the three towns on the Keys, the others being Layton and Key West, and it has its own police force, the small but modern Fisherman's Hospital, shopping plazas and restaurants, schools, several churches and fire and rescue squad. The Marathon Key Chamber of Commerce's Visitor Center is at MM 53.5.

The town still retains, how-ever, much of its nineteenth-century fishing village charm. Marathon, with its many resorts, makes an excellent base for ex-ploring the Keys because both the Lower Keys and Key West and the Upper Keys can easily be visited in very leisurely day trips.

The Arts

The **Marathon Community Theater** (☎ 743-0994) stages productions throughout the year, and the **Middle Keys' Concert Association** (☎ 289-1078) is also very active. There are a number of galleries on the island including the **Book Key and Gallery** (MM 53) which exhibits and sells oils and watercolours by local artists, open daily (☎ 743-5256), **Bougain-villea House**, 12421 Over-seas Highway, which features the work of local craftsman jewelers (☎ 743-0808), **Kennedy Studios** MM 48 (☎ 743-2040) which features local artists, and **Last Resort Art Collective,** MM 48.5 Faro Blanco, which is open daily and features local artists and sculptors.

The railway

When the Flagler railroad was being built, Marathon was a major supply depot and at one stage housed 3,000 workers. It is said the town got its name because, by the time they reached the island, their undertaking had become a marathon task. Marathon was the western terminus for the railroad for a time, and ferries and boats from Key West would dock at Knight Key to unload passengers and freight for the

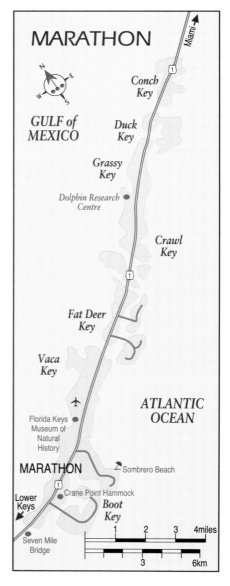

Bahia Honda State Park, Marathon

trains heading back to the mainland. There was also a ferry until 1937 plying between Marathon and No Name Key, 15 miles (24km) to the west in the Lower Keys.

Activities

There are charter fishing boats, marinas, dive centres and watersports. It is an important area for both commercial and recreational fishing. There are 12 miles of former bridges in the area which are now closed to motor traffic and now serve as fishing piers. There is a chance to see the sort of fish you might catch at **Captain Hook's Seaquarium** MM 50 (☎ 743-2444), where pools and tanks feature local species.

Wet Willy's Buccaneer Lodge Beach Hotel at MM 48.5 (☎ 743-9071) offers a wide range of watersports including sailing and windsurfing.

Sports

Offshore and a popular dive site is the wreck of the *Ivory Coast*, the remains of a slave ship which sank after running aground in 1853. Sombrero Reef, marked by a large tower with light, is another popular diving area, and you can explore the 188ft (57m) *Thunderbolt* sunk off Marathon, and now part of an artificial reef. There are several certified charter

Crane Point Hammock

Crane Point Hammock (MM 48), which includes The Museum of Natural History of the Florida Keys and Children's Museum (MM 50), has recently been acquired by the Florida Keys Land and Sea Trust. The wooded Hammock covers 63.5 acres (25 hectares) and is one of the most important botanical, archaeological and historical sites on the Keys.

It has a wide range of tropical vegetation, including 10 endangered plant and animal species, plus 160 native and 50 exotic plant varieties, and it is the last virgin palm hammock in North America.

There is a self-guiding interpretive Nature Trail which winds through mangrove, palm and hardwood hammocks, and passes a pit where ocean fossils have been exposed after thousands of years of rain and erosion.

The area contains evidence of pre-Columbian and prehistoric Bahamian artifacts. It was once the site of a large Indian village and a number of historically interesting structures. These include an 'Indian and hurricane-proof' home built with 2ft thick (0.6m) walls in the late 1800s.

Museums

The museum (☎ 743-9100) has a recreated coral reef cave, and fascinating displays about the Keys' early Indian settlers, pirates and wreckers.

There are exhibits from seventeenth-century shipwrecks, a collection of household artifacts from the Bahamas from the end of the nineteenth century, and it traces with artifacts the 5,000 year history of man's habitation of the region. It has the largest collection of ancient Keys' Indian remains on display anywhere, and another star attraction is a massive photograph of the region taken from space.

You can also visit the adjoining Florida Keys' Children's Museum, which explains the islands' natural history with interactive exhibits and displays.

The Florida Keys' Land and Sea Trust has now started work on expanding the complex by building a community education center, restored historic village and a marine science research and education center.

Crane Point Hammock and the museums are open Monday to Saturday from 9am to 5pm, and Sunday 12noon to 5pm. There is an admission charge for the museums.

boat captains available for diving, snorkelling, sailing, fishing and touring.

For those who prefer land sports, Marathon has an 18-hole championship golf course, which is open to members of country clubs. A club ID may be asked for.

Residents and visitors alike descend on the boat docks in the late afternoon to inspect the catches. The *Bounty Hunter*, one of the many charter fishing boats, is the only one on the Keys that the author knows of, to offer a no-fish no-pay guarantee. The world record for a great barracuda was set on the *Bounty Hunter* when a 58lb fish was landed (☎ 743-2446).

Other places of interest

The **Old Seven Mile Bridge** (MM 47) is now an historic monument, and the longest fishing pier in the world. The small island below Old Seven Mile Bridge, which runs parallel to the new structure, is **Pigeon Key**, which once housed Flagler's railroad workforce in the early 1900s, and it has changed little since then. It has been declared an historic site and is open to the public. It is worth a visit to be able to step back in time, before heading back into the twentieth century.

Continued on p.62...

Above: The charter fishing jetty at Vaca Key, Marathon
Below: There are lots of places where you can find peace and quiet like this!

*Awaiting the day's guests at
Quay Restaurant, Marathon*

EATING OUT
ON MARATHON & MIDDLE KEYS

Adventure Island (MM 54) $$
Seafood and American
Marathon
☎ 289-1742
Open all day.

Angler's (MM 48.5) $
American
Faro Blanco Resort
☎ 743-9018
Open for lunch.

Banana Cabana $-$$
Seafood and steaks
4590 Overseas Highway, Marathon
☎ 289-1232
Open for lunch and dinner.

Beach House Restaurant $-$$
Continental
Key Colony Beach
☎ 743-3939
Open for lunch and dinner, closed
Sunday.

Cantina (MM 61) $
Seafood and Mexican
Hawk's Cay Resort, Duck Key
☎ 743-7000
Open from early lunch to dinner.

Chef's $-$$
Seafood and steaks
Sombrero Resort, Marathon
☎ 743-4108
Open for breakfast and dinner,
closed Tuesday.

China American Garden $
Chinese
1622 Overseas Highway, Marathon
☎ 743-2140
Open for lunch and dinner, closed
Tuesday.

Cracked Conch Cafe $$
Seafood. Some of the best Seafood
in the Keys
4999 Overseas Highway, Marathon
☎ 743-CAFE

Crocodiles on the Water (MM 48)
$-$$
Seafood and steaks
End of 15 Street, Marathon
☎ 743-9018
Open for dinner.

Don Pedro (MM 53) $
Cuban and American
Marathon
☎ 743-5247
Open for dinner except Tuesday.

El Castillito $-$$
Seafood and Cuban
Marathon
☎ 743-7676
Open for dinner except Tuesday.

Golden Palace $-$$
Chinese
10877 Overseas Highway,
Marathon
☎ 289-0880
Open from lunch to dinner.

Hideaway Cafe, Rainbow Bend
Resort (MM 58) $$-$$$
Grassy Key
Award winning ocean-front
dinning. Continental
☎ 289-1554

Hurricane Raw Bar (MM 49.5) $-$$
Seafood
Marathon
☎ 743-5755
Open for lunch and dinner.

Jo-Jo's Restaurant (MM 60) $-$$
Seafood, steak and Italian
Grassy Key
☎ 289-0600
Open for lunch and dinner.

Key Colony Inn $-$$
Seafood and Italian
Key Colony Beach
Open for lunch and dinner.

The Landing Restaurant
(MM 53.5) $-$$
Seafood and Steaks
Key Colony Beach
☎ 289-0141
Open from early lunch to dinner.

Latigo Dinner Cruises
(MM 47.5) $$-$$$
Sunset cruises with gourmet dinner
11th St. Marathon
☎ 289-1066

Pancho Villa's Steakhouse
(MM 48) $-$$
Seafood, steaks and Tex-Mex
Marathon
☎ 289-1629
Open all day.

Paradise Cafe (MM 68.5) $
Italian
Long Key
☎ 664-4900
Open all day.

Perry's Seafood Restaurant $$
Steak and seafood
6900 Overseas Highway, Marathon
☎ 743-3447
Open from early lunch to dinner.

Porto Cayo (MM 61) $$
Seafood and Italian
Hawk's Cay Resort, Duck Key
☎ 743-7000
Open for dinner, closed Monday.

The Quay (MM 54) $$
Gourmet
seafood and steaks
Marathon
☎ 289-1810
Open from early lunch to dinner.

The Ship's Pub (MM 61) $$
Seafood and steaks
Hawk's Cay Resort, Duck Key
☎ 743-7000
Open for dinner.

Shucker's Raw Bar and Grill
(MM 47) $$
Seafood and steak
11th Street, Marathon
☎ 743-8686
Open from lunch to dinner.

Stout's Restaurant $
Family fare
84 Street and Overseas Highway
☎ 743-6437
Open weekdays for breakfast and
lunch, and dinner Wed to Friday.

Village Cafe
(MM 50) $-$$
Seafood, steak and Italian
☎ 743-9090
Open all day.

Wobbly Crab Restaurant $
Home cooking
5230 Overseas Highway
☎ 743-3417
Open for breakfast, early lunch
and dinner.

There are many old Conch Houses and the area is being restored by the Pigeon Key Foundation (☎ 289-0025). A mini-passenger train runs along the old bridge to Pigeon Key.

The centre-span of the Old Seven Mile Bridge was dropped into the ocean and used to create an artificial reef, and this is now a very popular dive site. The span was part of the bridge built by Flagler for his Overseas Railroad, which was destroyed in the 1935 hurricane. In April, Marathon Key hosts the annual Seven Mile Bridge Run which attracts a field of about 1,500.

The route then crosses **Seven Mile Bridge**, opened in 1982 and the longest segmental bridge in the world, to the Lower Keys. The bridge was built in sections in Tampa and carried by barge to the keys. There are 288 sections each 135ft (41m) long.

Nightlife

Angler's, Candlelight Bar, Key Colony Beach, The Landing, The Quay and the Ship's Pub.

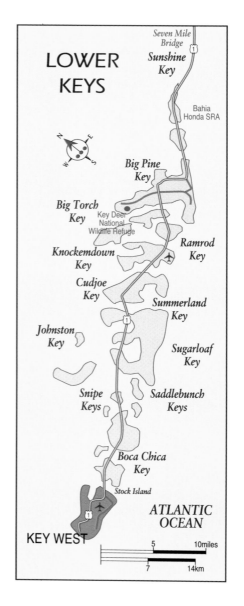

62

THE LOWER KEYS

The Lower Keys run from Little Duck Key to Stock Island, although this is now really an overflow for Key West. Many geologists also believe that the Lower Keys, because of the rock formations, are an extension of the Appalachian Chain which runs up much of the eastern seaboard of the United States.

Seven Mile Bridge crosses Little Duck Key and Missouri Key with the Veterans' Memorial Park, to **Sunshine Key** (MM39). This small 75-acre (30 hectare) island used to be called Ohio Key, but changed its name for marketing purposes and now has a large campground. It offers a wide range of facilities and recreational activities.

Right: Perky Bat Tower, Sugarloaf Key

Below: Mangrove Swamp at Ramrod Key

BAHIA HONDA KEY

Bahia Honda means 'deep bay', and is interesting both geologically and botanically. **Bahia Honda State Park** (MM 37) is 6 miles (9.6km) north-east of Big Pine Key and covers all 635 acres (254 hectares) of the island. The park entrance is at MM 36.9 of US 1 on Bahia Honda Key.

The island has lovely sand beaches and has consistently been voted by several US magazines as among the top ten beaches in the country. There are lush tropical hardwood forests, with dense thicket

undergrowth inland. The park is also noted for its rare flowers, many of them from the Caribbean such as Jamaican morning glory and wild dilly.

The self-guiding **Silver Palm Nature Trail** follows the shore past yellow satinwood, gumbo limbo and silver palms, and the tidal lagoon at the end of Sandspur Beach. This is a great place to canoe because you can paddle your way among the mangroves which surround the lagoon.

It is also very good for bird-watching. You can see brown pelicans, double-crested cormorants, many species of herons, white-crowned pigeons, laughing gull, sanderling, smooth billed anis and osprey year-round. In the winter there are also ibis, sandpipers, terns and ring-billed gulls, and in the autumn you might spot migrating warblers, black-whiskered vireos and mangrove cuckoos. There are rangerguided walks and daily snorkel trips to the reefs of the **Looe Key National Marine Sanctuary**. (☎ 872-2353)

The park offers three camping areas, vacation cabins, picnicking, seafishing, hiking and swimming in both the Atlantic Ocean and Florida Bay. There is also a dive shop, boat ramp and refreshments.

The park is popular and access may be temporarily restricted when it gets too busy. The tarpon fishing here is among the best in Florida, and many rare species of birds can be seen including osprey, reddish egret and great white heron.

The original Flagler Bridge is off the southwestern peninsula, and is now a national historic site. There are great views of the sweep of both Florida Bay and the Gulf of Mexico from the new Bahia Honda Bridge (MM36).

BIG PINE KEY

Big Pine Key is the largest of the Lower Keys and one of the few with a permanent source of fresh water. It is an interesting island to explore because it is in sharp contrast to the resort of Marathon to the east and Key West to the west.

Much of the island is natural and near-wilderness country. As such, it is very popular with campers, nature lovers and those who want to enjoy the many recreational opportunities the land and water offer.

Visit the **Lower Keys Chamber of Commerce Visitor Center** at MM 31. There are 15 campgrounds to choose from in the Lower Keys, and while prices are slightly higher in Florida elsewhere, the amenities are excellent, and most are located by the water with boat ramps and docks. Many also offer planned activities for guests and host fish fries, lobster feasts and holiday festivities.

Highway 940 runs north from US1 and offers access to **No Name Key** to the east and the many keys to the north, such as Howe Key and Annette Key.

The island has large areas of the stunted pines which are typical of the Keys and is fringed with mangrove swamps. It also has an area of tropical hardwood with species such as gumbo lim-bo and poisonwood. Extensive mudflats are exposed at low tide which attract large numbers of wading birds, including the beautiful roseate spoonbill.

The Blue Hole, a former quarry, is the largest body of freshwater in the Keys, and an important fresh water alligator habitat with self-guiding walking trail just over a mile (1.6km) further north on Key Deer Boulevard. The viewing platform overlooks a disused quarry. The **Jack C Watson**

Key Deer National Wildlife Refuge

Key Deer National Wildlife Refuge covers 8,005 acres (3,200 hectares) on Big Pine Key and includes many of the smaller keys to the north. It was established to protect the small and rare Florida Key white-tailed deer, which is no larger than a medium-sized dog.

In the late 1940s there were believed to be fewer than forty of these deer in the wild. Numbers recovered to about 400 in the 1970s, but the latest estimate puts the population at under 300, two-thirds of which live on Big Pine Key.

You can visit the nature preserve at the west end of Watson Boulevard about 1.7 miles (2.7km) past the refuge headquarters in the Big Pine Shopping Center (☎ 872-2239) which is open Monday to Friday from 8am to 5pm.

The best time to spot the tiny deer is in the early evening, when they feed in the trees by the side of the road. Drive with great care and do not feed the deer, as this attracts them to the road, and many are killed by cars every year.

The refuge is also a good place to view turtles, and to spot migrating birds. More than 256 species of birds live in or travel through the area on migration, including mangrove cuckoos, roseate spoonbills, bald eagles and peregrine falcons. The refuge is open daily during daylight hours.

Above: South of Shark Channel, Sugarloaf Key

Below: For a different perspective, take a scenic flight out of Sugarloaf Key

Wildlife Trail begins a quarter of a mile (0.4km) north of Blue Hole on Key Deer Boulevard. **Watson's Hammock** (MM 31.5 –28.5) also has a number of primitive trails through tropical forests of poison wood, gumbo limbo, guava, acacia and strangler fig. You can pick up brochures for Blue Hole and the Watson Trail at the refuge headquarters.

Coupon Bight State Aquatics Preserve (MM 31.5–28.5) separates and protects the area between the mainland and the oceanside peninsula ☎ 872-2411.

Great White Heron National Refuge effectively covers all the Lower Keys and protects North America's largest wading bird, but you can best visit it on Big Pine Key between MM 28.5 and 31.5. The area, established in 1938, is visited by thousands of migrating and nesting birds every year and offers protection for a number of rare and endangered species ☎ 872-2239.

Summerland Key (MM 25) has become very popular in the last few years with a lot of development. There is a post office and a small airstrip. Monte's Restaurant and Fish Market at MM 25 is excellent ☎ 745-3731 .

Cudjoe Key (MM 23) covers 3,300 acres (1,320 hectares)

Looe Key National Marine Sanctuary

Looe Key National Marine Sanctuary (☎ 872-2411), south of Big Pine Key, is a noted shallow dive and snorkelling site with spectacular coral formations, sea fans, deep submarine canyons and shoals of multi-coloured tropical fish. It is named after HMS Looe, a British frigate that ran aground during a storm in 1744. It is a protected reef area.

Spearfishing, coral and shell collecting were banned in 1981 and the area now offers one of the most undisturbed dive sites in the Caribbean. It is exceptional because the shallow waters make it available to the most novice snorkellers, yet there are still a host of things to attract the most serious scuba divers. Many charter boats offer night dives, and for those who prefer not to get their feet wet, there are regular glass-bottomed boat cruises.

It is also home to one of the world's strangest musical events, the Lower Keys Underwater Music Festival. There is also excellent offshore fishing for tarpon, tuna, sailfish, bonefish, snook, dolphin (dorado) and snapper.

Big business flops

Sugarloaf Key (MM 20) is noted for its strange shape and the even stranger Perky Bat Tower, 30ft (10m) high at MM 17 and built in 1929 as suitable for migrating bats. The aim was to attract bats to the island who would then eat up all the mosquitoes.

The project was the idea of fishing lodge owner Richter Clyde Perky, whose guests were constantly troubled by the insects. The bat hotel was modelled on one in Texas, and the tower was filled with foul smelling guano as bat bait.

It was a spectacular failure and not a single bat turned up, but the tower is now on the National Register of Historic Places and has been restored by the Historic Key West Preservation Board.

In 1910 a Sponge Farm was established on the island by C W Chase, an Englishman, but his sponges were almost always stolen at night, and he finally sold out, to none other than Mr Perky!

although it does not have a large population. Cudjoe Key Road runs from US 1 to the north of the Key, and was built in 1960 to reach the US air force missile tracking station.

The station is home to **Fat Albert**, the massive white ballon that can usually be seen in the sky over the Key. You can drive down to the coast in the direction of the blimp, and a second is usually anchored on the ground. The approach road to the government facility is restricted.

Loggerhead Key used to be the home of hundreds of rhesus monkeys. They were brought from India in 1972 and the idea was to let them breed and so establish a supply of animals for laboratory experiments.

Highway 939 runs from US 1 round the southern shore of the Key before heading inland to re-connect with the Overseas Highway at Perky.

The highway then crosses the water to **Saddlebunch Keys**, a delightful cluster of islands, whose main inhabitants are the mangrove trees, although there is a US Navy communications facility north of the highway, and a residential development to the south.

Big Coppitt (MM 11) and **Rockland Key** are largely populated by the families of servicemen stationed on the Naval Air Base on neighbouring **Boca Chica Key** (MM 6). The Air Station is used as a training base for carrier aircraft.

EATING OUT ON THE LOWER KEYS

Inexpensive $ Moderate $$ Expensive $$$

Bobalu Southern Cafe (MM 10)
$-$$
American–Creole
Boca Chica
☎ 296-1664
Open daily.

Boondocks (MM 27.5) $
American
Ramrod Key
☎ 872-0022
Open all day.

China Gardens $-$$
Chinese
Winn Dixie Shopping Center
Big Pine
☎ 872-8861

Galley Grill $
Seafood and steaks
Summerland Key
☎ 745-3446
Open from breakfast to
lunch and dinner.

K.D.'s (MM 30.5) $-$$
Great steaks and seafood
Big Pine
☎ 872-2314

Little Palm Island
(MM 28.5) $$-$$$
Great gourmet food, great value,
French and Caribbean
Little Torch Key
☎ 872-2524

Open for lunch and dinner,
reservations recommended.
Access by boat only.

Mangrove Mama's (MM 20) $$
Seafood and Caribbean
Sugarloaf Key
☎ 745-3030
Open for lunch and dinner
daily except Tuesday.

Monte's Restaurant and Seafood
Market (MM 25) $
Seafood and American
Summerland Key
☎ 745-3731
Open all day.

No Name Pub $-$$
American
Watson Blvd, Big Pine
☎ 872-9155
Open for lunch and dinner.

Raimondo's Ristorante
Italiano (MM 21) $$
Italian
Cudjoe Key
☎ 745-9999
Open daily 5 to 10pm.

NIGHTLIFE

Cedar Inn and No Name Pub

3. Key West

Key West is 150 miles (242km) south-west of Miami, and is the southernmost city in the continental United States. Its unique atmosphere is partly because, being only 90 miles (145km) across the sea from Cuba, it is nearer to Havana than Miami and has a strong Caribbean influence. Its remoteness has long attracted groups in the past who, for one reason or another, were not considered mainstream.

Over the years it has been the home of Spanish conquistadors, pirates, New England mariners and European royalty. Today, it has a strong gay population, is popular with artists and writers, and attracts about 1.5 million visitors each year.

It is most famous as the home of writer Ernest Hemingway, and there must be something in the air that stimulates writers to greatness. Ten Pulitzer Prizes have been awarded to writers who have lived on Key West, and more than 100 published

Above: Conch Tour Train

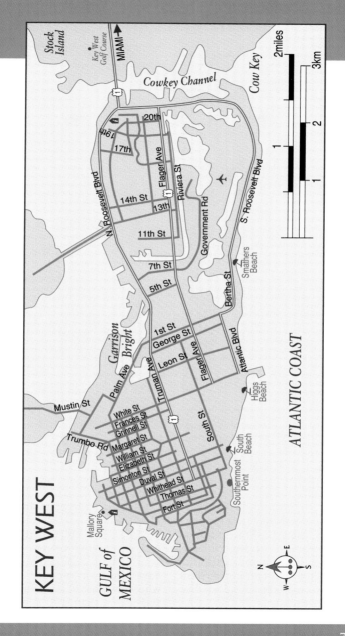

KEY WEST

GULF of MEXICO

ATLANTIC COAST

Stock Island

Key West Golf Course

MIAMI

Cowkey Channel

Cow Key

20th
19th
17th
14th St
13th
11th St
7th St
5th St

Flager Ave
Riviera St
Government Rd

N Roosevelt Blvd
S. Roosevelt Blvd

Smathers Beach
Bertha St

Garrison Bright

Palm Ave
Mustin St

1st St
George St
Leon St

Truman Ave
Flager Ave
Atlantic Blvd

Higgs Beach

Trumbo Rd

White St
Frances St
Grinnell St
Margaret St
William St
Elizabeth St
Simonton St
Duval St
Whithead St
Thomas St
Fort St

South St

South Beach
Southernmost Point

Mallory Square

N
W E
S

2miles
3km
2
1
1

authors live full or part-time on the island.

Key West has boasted many other famous residents such as Thomas Edison, Elizabeth Bishop, Lou Gehrig, Harry Truman and Tennessee Williams. It is still popular with writers, artists and the famous, and celebrity-spotting is an island pastime.

BACKGROUND

The island city has a resident population of about 24,800, and is only 3.5 miles by 1 mile (5.6 by 1.6km).

It was originally called **Cayo Hueso** (Bone Island) by the first Spanish settlers, because of the number of bones found on the beach. It is not known if these were the bones of sailors shipwrecked on the reefs, or settlers who were killed by the Indians.

Key West was once the home of many cigar factories founded by emigres from Cuba, and was noted for the canning of turtle meat which was another major industry.

STYLE

Today there are frequent reminders of its colourful industry and past, with fine old and historic buildings, and many styles of architecture from West Indian gingerbread to classic Victorian.

Wrecks and treasures

Key West became popular with pirates and privateers because of the heavily-laden Spanish treasure galleons which sailed past on their way back to Spain from the gold and silver mines of the New World.

Rumours that huge fortunes lie on the ocean floor still attract divers and treasure-hunters in their tens of thousands. These rumours do have some basis in fact, because it is known, for instance, that in 1733 a Spanish fleet was hit by a fierce storm off Plantation Key and the ships were swept south to founder on the reefs.

Legend has it that the fleet was carrying a huge treasure in gold and silver. Over the past few decades, hundreds of millions of dollars-worth of treasure, in the form of gold, silver and jewels, has been recovered from the offshore waters.

Other popular dive sites include the 65ft (20m) long *Joe's Tug*, which sits upright on the seabed surrounded by coral

The architecture is just one of the pleasing aspects of Key West. Most of the wooden buildings are built in a style referred to as Conch, or Bahamian. This is really a mixture

formations. It is the home of a large jewfish nicknamed Elvis by local divers.

The *Cayman Salvage Master*, an 185ft (52m) Coast Guard buoy tender, is one of the Keys' most visited wrecks.

Many other ships foundered in the shallow waters off Key West, and some of these may not have been accidents. Wreckers could make fortunes salvaging the cargoes of ships which came to grief on the rocks, and it was not unknown for lights to be positioned on the reefs so that ships would be misled into thinking they had a safe passage.

Because the local waters carried so much shipping, a series of forts was built on Key West with Fort Zachary Taylor guarding the island's west shore, East Martello Tower and West Martello Tower along the south shore, and Fort Jefferson National Monument, the largest link in America's nineteenth-century coastal defences, 70 miles (113km) west of Key West in the Dry Tortugas.

elaborate scroll-cut work on balconies, under eaves and under gables. Wrought iron railings were also popular, and these features continue to add a special Caribbean charm.

TOURISM

Tourism is now by far the biggest income earner, followed by commercial and sport fishing. There are about 60 deep-sea charter boats and 15 flat-fishing skiffs, as well as two large party fishing boats. Charter boats usually cater to groups of four to six, and charge about $550 all included. Light tackle boats may accommodate fewer passengers and charge less, and large party boats offer good value, as you can enjoy a day's fishing for about $30 a person.

STOCK ISLAND

Stock Island is generally considered part of Key West as it is the neighbouring island connected by a 159ft (48m) bridge. It gets its name because it was used to rear cattle and then pigs, before Key West overspill developments, both residential and commercial, took over.

Stock Island is home of the **Key West Resort Golf Course** ☎ 294-5232. It is an 18-hole championship course designed by Rees Jones and open to the

of styles, and many of the buildings were constructed by ship's carpenters. The town adopted gingerbread in the 1850s, and it became very fashionable to incorporate

Continued on p.76...

73

Above: Mallory Square
Below: Sloppy Joe's Bar, made famous by Hemingway
Opposite: Hemingway's House

The Conch Republic

Many long-time residents on Key West refer to themselves as 'conchs' (pronounced konks), and in the second half of April, there is a rather zany series of events and activities to celebrate the Conch Republic.

It all stems from a move by the US Border Patrol to set up a border checkpoint north of Key Largo on 20 April, 1982. Keys residents argued that if the border was north of Key Largo, then everywhere south must be outside the United States and so on 23 April they announced the independent Conch Republic, and ran up the Republic's new flag in Mallory Square.

When the United States refused to recognise the new republic, the Conchs declared 'war' on the US and then immediately surrendered and applied for foreign aid. The annual 'Independence' celebrations are a time for partying and parades, both on land and water, and the raising of the Conch flag at Fort Zachary Taylor accompanied by a cannon salvo. It is mixture of Mardi-Gras and Carnival, and great fun.

public. There is also the Florida Keys Community College and the **Tennessee Williams Fine Arts Center,** ☎ 296-1520, which presents opera, dance, classical and chamber music concerts, and entertains national and international companies performing everything from Shakespeare to current Broadway hits. Tennessee Williams' House at 1431 Duncan Street, Key West, is not open to the public but can be viewed from the outside.

The 11-acre Botanical Garden just off College Road at MM 5 Bayside, features exotic and native plants, walking trails, gazebo and picnic area.

ROAD LAYOUT

The Overseas Highway divides when it reaches Key West.

You can turn right on to **North Roosevelt Boulevard** which runs around the northern coast to the marina on Garrison Bight. It then continues westerly as Truman Avenue which runs into Old Town.

If you turn left on to **South Roosevelt Boulevard**, you follow the south coast between the Key West International Airport and the East Martello Tower Museum and Gallery, Salt Ponds and County Beach. Some of the area around the Salt Ponds make up **Riggs Wildlife and Bird Reserve**.

The road then connects with Bertha Street and runs north into First Street which connects with North Roosevelt

Boulevard at the marina. You can continue along the south coast by following Atlantic Boulevard to the White Street fishing pier and the West Martello Tower, and past the Smathers City, and Clarence Higgs Public Beaches.

Just before the pier, you can visit **Indigenous Park** and wander through the many different species of tropical trees and plants, all of which have identification labels, and you can then enjoy the lovely **Joe Allen Garden Center** at the West Martello Tower.

Old Town

Atlantic Boulevard connects with South Street, and if you turn left you can take any of the roads off it on the right – Simonton, Duval or Whitehead Streets – into the old town. If you go to the end of Whitehead Street, you are at the Southernmost Point of the continental United States, and at what most people consider is the end of the Overseas Highway.

Street signs are not always obvious in Key West. They may be on yellow sign posts at the street corner, may be painted

continued on p.88...

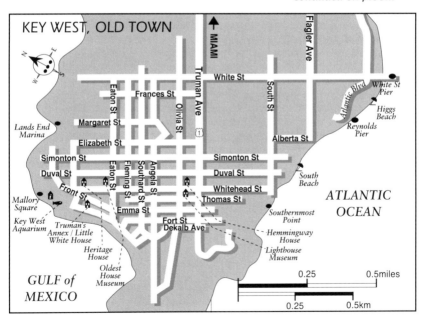

KEY WEST, OLD TOWN

MIAMI

Flagler Ave

White St

Eaton St

Frances St

Truman Ave

Olivia St

South St

Atlantic Blvd

White St Pier

Higgs Beach

Lands End Marina

Margaret St

Reynolds Pier

Elizabeth St

Alberta St

Simonton St

Simonton St

Eaton St

Fleming St

Southard St

Angela St

Duval St

Duval St

Front St

Whitehead St

South Beach

Mallory Square

Thomas St

Emma St

ATLANTIC OCEAN

Key West Aquarium

Truman's Annex / Little White House

Fort St
Dekalb Ave

Southernmost Point

Heritage House

Hemmingway House

Oldest House Museum

Lighthouse Museum

GULF of MEXICO

0.25   0.5miles

0.25   0.5km

A Short Walking Tour of

There is an excellent historic and architectural self-guiding tour called the Pelican Path which is easy to follow because you simply look for the pelican signs which are mounted everywhere. The path takes in almost every building of historic and architectural interest in Old Town, and you can pick up a brochure from the Visitor Center. The following is a shorter version, taking in the main points of interest in Old Town which is bordered by Whitehead and White Streets.

Mallory Square with the Key West Hospitality House, makes a good place to start and end your walk. It is also home to two of Key West's four theatres, the Art Center, the recently-opened Key West Shipwreck Historeum, and the city's famous Aquarium.

Key West Bight, off Mallory Square is a good place to take a mini-cruise. There are glass-bottomed boats, and vessels available for fishing and diving charters.

Back on land, enjoy the shops and views and visit Pirates Alley, which runs off the square and where you can still see cigars being hand-rolled, and then head for Greene Street and the Wreckers and Mel Fisher Maritime Heritage Museum.

Running south off Greene Street is Whitehead Street and the Audubon House. Just off Whitehead Street, in Caroline Street, you can visit the Curry Mansion and Patterson House, the finest example of Queen Anne architecture on the island, and Kemp House at No 601, the Conch-style at its best.

The Post Office, Lighthouse Museum and Ernest Hemingway House are all on Whitehead Street. Whitehead Street was one of five military roads built by Commodore David Porter, commander of the West India Squadron posted to the island in 1822. The roads ran the width of the island, but Whitehead is the only one that remains.

Duval Street runs parallel inland from Whitehead Street, and is known as the longest street in the world because it runs from one ocean to another – the Atlantic to the Gulf of Mexico! It is also Key West's main street, and in the heart of Key West's Old Town.

Visit Fast Buck Freddie's, the island's department store, and St. Paul's Church (No 401), the oldest Episcopal church in the South Florida Diocese. The first service was held on Christmas Day,

OLD TOWN, KEY WEST

1832, although the present church, built in 1916, is the fourth on the site. The oldest religious building on the island is the Methodist Church on Eaton Street, which was built from local stone in 1877. Also in Duval Street is the San Carlos Opera House (No 516), a beautiful example of late nineteenth-century Cuban architecture.

Parallel with it is Simonton Street, where you can visit Key West Handprint Fabrics, tour the factory and watch the garments being designed, sewn and modelled. Then head back down Simonton Street past the shops towards Mallory Square. Turn left into Eaton Street and on its corner with Duval Street is St. Paul's Episcopal Church, which was destoyed three times by hurricanes until rebuilt in brick in 1919.

In Front Street, which ends at the waterside, you can visit the Little White House Museum, so named because it was the summer house of President Harry Truman in the 1940s. There are guided tours, and it is even possible to overnight in the Presidential Suites.

Take time to visit the Sawyer Building (No 400), built in 1866 after a fire had destroyed many of town's buildings. Irish bricklayers from Boston were brought down for the construction. The first floor was the US District Court for some time.

Also on Front Street is the ornamental Old Post Office built in 1891, which also served as Court House and Customs House, and the Coast Guard Building, built in 1856 as a Navy Coaling Station. It was used during the Civil War as the headquarters of the East Coast Blockade Squadron.

Front Street is also famous for its many restaurants which look out over the harbour, and for the marina at Lands End Village where many of the shrimp and commercial fishing boats unload their catches. You can also visit Key West Fragrances on Front Street, which has a wide range of beautiful and unusual scents; then return to Mallory Square to enjoy a great Key West sunset.

Note: Bicycles and mopeds can be rented at a number of locations. These also make ideal forms of transport for exploring the city and neighbouring Keys.

on the base of street lamps, or they may not be present at all. It does not really matter though, because if you learn the layout of the city and the main streets, you can not get lost.

PLACES OF INTEREST

AUDUBON HOUSE AND GARDENS

205 Whitehead Street
☎ 294-2116
This beautifully restored house built in 1812 contains original John James Audubon engravings and has eighteenth and nineteenth century furnishings from around the world, as was the style at that time.

There is also a gallery of porcelain bird sculptures. The artist was a visitor to the house in the 1830s, which was owned by John H Geiger, sea captain, harbour pilot and master wrecker. Audubon would frequently be out in the mangrove swamps at 3am and work until the early hours the next day, capturing the images of the birds and plants in their natural habitat.

The house was bought in the 1960s by Miami businessman Mitchell Wolfson who, after completely restoring it, dedicated it as a public museum to be named Audubon House. The house is also of great interest because it contains the original hinges, hardware and wood used by ships' carpenters in its construction. It took architects two years to research and complete the restoration, and there is not a single metal nail used, as all fastenings are with wooden pegs.

The restoration was also of note because it sparked off a preservation movement led by a pair of Old Town merchants, who teamed together to renovate fifteen buildings along the 600 block of historic Duval Street, and this trend continues throughout the city. There are tours of the house and gardens. Open daily 9.30am to 5pm. Admission charge.

BAHAMA VILLAGE

Showcasing Key West's Caribbean heritage with a Bahamian marketplace, shops, ethnic restaurants and galleries. You can also visit the Lofton B. Sands African-Bahamian Center at 324 Truman Ave. ☎ 295-7337.

OLD TOWN

A lively area in the heart of Old Town with bars, restaurants, shops, public pool and playground, and the home of the annual **Goombay Festival**.

BEACHES

Public beaches, which close at 11pm, are found at **Smathers Beach**, **S Roosevelt Boulevard** near the airport, **Higgs Beach** on Atlantic Boulevard, **South**

Beach, at the end of Duval Street, and **Fort Zachary Taylor** with access though Southard Street. **Dog Beach** is next to Louie's Backyard Restaurant and is popular with pet owners who like to swim with their pooches.

CONCH TOUR TRAIN

☎ 294-5161
A 90-minute conducted tour which starts at Front Street, Mallory Square, and takes in scores of places of interest on Key West, including historic sites, old conch homes and architecture, along its 4.5 mile (7km) route. It has carried more than 10 million passengers. Tours leave on the hour between 9am and 4pm.

CURRY MANSION

Caroline Street ☎ 294-5349
A National Register 1899 Victorian mansion, with twenty-two elegant rooms, packed with antiques, rare Tiffany glass and other furnishings. Lovely porches and verandas, and the Widow's Walk.

It was built by the son of William Curry, reputedly Florida's first millionaire. The house is said to have been a replica of a property that he and his wife had seen while honeymooning in Paris. Open daily 10am to 5pm. Admission charge.

THE CUSTOMS HOUSE

Old Town ☎ 296-3913
Built in the heart of Old Town in 1891, the Customs House was the headquarters for most of the federal services on the Keys including US Customs, US Lighthouse Service, US District Court, US Internal Revenue Service and the Post Office. The imposing red brick building is the finest example of Romanesque Revival architecture in Florida, and efforts to save the building from private development have been successful. It has now been bought by the State and houses the **Museum of Art and History**, open daily 9am-5.30pm.

DONKEY MILK HOUSE MUSEUM

613 Eaton Street ☎ 296-1866
A restored 1866 Greek Revival-style house in Old Town. It gets its name from the alley at the back where donkeys (which pulled the milk carts) were kept. The house was built in the 1860s and has lovely Spanish tile floors, painted ceilings and period furnishings and fixtures. Open daily 10am to 5pm. Admission charge.

EAST MARTELLO FORT MUSEUM AND ART GALLERY

South Roosevelt Boulevard ☎ 296-3913
Now the home of **Key West Art and Historical Society**, the thir-

teen vaulted rooms with brick arches, house folk art displays, and historic artifacts found on the islands. It is a good place to learn about the history of the island, with old photographs and special displays about the cigar and sponge industries and the railroad era.

The Art Gallery exhibits the work of local artists, and displays the colourful, primitive wood carvings and paintings of native Key West artist Mario Sanchez. It is worth climbing the 48 steps to the top of the **Citadel** for the views over the island and ocean beyond.

Although construction did not begin until 1861 the east and west Martello forts were

authorised by Congress in 1844, before the Civil War, to protect Fort Taylor. New military equipment quickly made them obsolete, and they were never completed — only the first ten feet (3m) or so of the red brickwork remains.

The Martello towers, similar to medieval structures found in Europe, had lower outer walls encircling a waterless moat, and tall thick-walled tower — the Citadel. Both have been well restored. Open daily from 9.30am to 5pm. Admission charge.

Left: Lighthouse Museum

Above : Bahama Village

Opposite: Hoping for one more as the sun sets at Faro Blanco

The **West Martello Tower**, just over two miles (3km) to the west, is now home of the **Key West Garden Club**. The wonderful tropical gardens have examples of island plant life. Only the lower level courses of the red brick tower remain, but if you look at the West Martello Tower you can see dents in the brickwork – a relic of the time when the tower was used as a target by the gunners at Fort Taylor. West Martello Tower and Gardens are open daily and admission is free.

EATON STREET THEATRE

☎ 296-3030
Seasonal productions.

ERNEST HEMINGWAY HOME AND MUSEUM

907 Whitehead Street
☎ 294-1575

The author's home from 1931 to 1961, and where he wrote many of his famous works. He lived there with his wife Pauline for ten years from 1931 and did not sell the house until shortly before his death in Idaho in July, 1961. He was awarded the Nobel Prize for Literature in 1954.

Registered as a National Historic Landmark, the beautiful Spanish Colonial-style house was built in local stone in 1851 by Asa Tift, the architect of the Confederate Navy. It was very unusual in that many

rooms had fireplaces, and one of the only cellars in the island.

The house and its furnishings including rugs, tiles, chandeliers and furniture from around the world, are exactly as they were left by Hemingway. It is almost as if the author is just away on a trip, and will return in a day or two.

When Hemingway and his wife moved in, they built the city's first swimming pool in the spacious grounds, where peacocks and cats roamed. Pauline had the pool built at a cost of $20,000 while Hemingway was away on one of his trips. On his return, and hearing how much the pool cost, he is said to have taken a one cent coin from his pocket, saying 'Here, take the last penny I've got.' His wife had the coin embedded in cement at the head of the pool, where it can still be seen. Hemingway loved game fishing and had his own boat *Pilar*.

You can visit the writer's study where he wrote *Death in the Afternoon, For Whom the Bell Tolls, Green Hills of Africa* and many other books. *To Have and To Have Not* is set in and near Key West in the Depression. The author's life is detailed in photographs and exhibits, and you can also see the descendants of the author's famous six-toed cats, who still frequent the house and gardens. Many of the trees and shrubs were planted by the nature-loving writer. Open daily 9am to 5pm. Admission charge.

FIREBALL

Duvall Street ☎ 296-6293
Glass-bottomed boat sightseeing trips, day trips over the coral reefs and sunset cruises.

HENRY FLAGLER'S OVERSEA RAILWAY MUSEUM

Flager Street-Caroline Street
☎ 295-3562
Explore the history and legacy of Henry Flagler's East Coast Railroad Key West Extension.

FORT ZACHARY TAYLOR STATE HISTORIC SITE

☎ 292-6713
Has an interpretive centre and museum.

The trapezoid-shaped fort, completed after 21 years work in 1866, was named in honour of the country's 12th President. It was at one time known as Fort Forgotten, because it was buried under tons of sand, and the site at one stage was even considered for a sewage treatment plant.

In 1968 Howard England, a Key West resident, historian and architect for the Key West Naval Base, literally started to dig up the fort. Using a shovel he and his two sons worked on weekends to move the covering sand.

Best beach

At Fort Taylor, there are facilities for swimming, picnics, snorkelling and sea fishing from the 51-acre (20 hectares) man-made beach next to the fort which was originally surrounded by water. The beach, with its clear water, white sand and tree-shaded picnic tables, has made Fort Taylor the top beach on Key West. It is open daily from dawn to dusk.

The fort's south side was exposed first, including two batteries built within the walls in 1898. Over the next decade, Howard England and a growing band of volunteers, excavated thousands of cannonballs, bullets and cannon from seven of the 24 gun rooms.

Although Fort Taylor was never fired on, it was occupied by the Union Army during the Civil War, and contains the largest collection of Civil War cannon in the United States. The fort was the home base for a successful blockade of Confederate ships, and some historians say the blockade reduced the war by a year.

The Fort Taylor State Recreation Area was opened to the public in the summer of 1985. The fort annually receives tens of thousands of visitors who can go on conducted tours, examine the armaments and visit the museum.

Historic Seaport at Key West Bight. A half mile stretch of shops, restaurants and bars.

GALLERIES

There are scores of galleries to explore on the island. Of note are the Gingerbread Square Gallery, 1207 Duval Street, which features internationally-acclaimed local artists such as Sal Salinero and John Kiraly, David Scott Meier Gallery, 614 Duval Street, which exhibits the work of local artists, the Harrison Gallery, 825 White Street, which features the sculptures of Helen Harrison, and the Island Arts Gallery, an artists' cooperative at 1128 Duval Street. The Joy Gallery, 429 Caroline Street, Les Deux J Gallery, 1130 Duval Street, Key West Art Centre, 301 Front Street, Kudu Gallery, 1208 Duval Street, Lucky Street Gallery, 919 Duval Street, The Gallery on Greene, 606 Greene Street and Wyland Gallery, 717 Duval Street, all feature the work of local artists.

GARRISON BIGHT MARINA

☎ 294-3093

On the north shore, off Eisenhower Drive, is the charter boat dock. There are all sorts of boats for hire, with or without crews, and it is a great place to visit late in the afternoon if you want some fish for supper, as the fishing charters will be docking laden with their catches.

HAITIAN ART COMPANY

Frances Street
Old Town ☎ 296-8932
One of the largest and finest collections of Haitian art in the United States – painting, wood

The Pier House sits right on the beach

and metal sculptures and paper mache — open daily 10am to 6pm.

JESSIE PORTER'S HERITAGE HOUSE MUSEUM

Caroline Street ☎ 296-3573
You can tour the former home of Jessie Porter Newton and six generations of the Porter family, one of the most eminent in Key West.

The oldest part of the house dates from the 1830s and was built for an English sea captain. The property has many family antiques and artifacts spanning the generations.

In the gardens is the Robert Frost Cottage. Frost was a poet, family friend and frequent winter visitor. Taped recordings of his poetry are played in the gardens. Open daily from 10am to 5pm.

HIGGS BEACH

A popular area with children's playground, pier, sailboat rentals, picnic tables and barbecue grills.

Indigenous Park is a six acre bird Sanctuary and wildlife refuge near the junction of White Street and Atlantic Blvd.

KEY WEST AQUARIUM

Junction of Wall and Whitehead Streets in Mallory Square ☎ 296-2051
Opened in 1932, the aquarium was the Florida Keys' first tourist attraction. It was also the first open-air aquarium in the United States. There is a 50,000-gallon tank featuring a near-shore mangrove environment showing the wealth and variety of tropical and game fish, sea turtles and birds it supports. There are daily tours at 11am, 1pm, 3pm and 4.30pm and you can watch the sharks, rays and turtles being fed as guides explain about the habits and habitats of the different creatures. There is a touch tank and in another, the sharks can be petted and fed by hand. It is open daily from 10am to 6pm.

KEY WEST BIGHT MARINA

☎ 296-3838
Offers charter boats, jet skis, jet boats, parasailing and other watersports.

KEY WEST BUTTERFLY & NATURE CONSERVANCY

1316 Duval Street
☎ 305-296-2988
One of the only three major butterfly facilities in Florida and featuring a 5,000 sq. ft. glass domed tropical butterfly habitat, housing up to 1,200 butterflies from 50 species.

THE KEY WEST CEMETERY

☎ 292-6718
The cemetery is like the city itself – unique – and well worth a visit both for its historical impor-

tance, and the wry humour inscribed on many of the gravestones.

One headstone bears the epitaph 'I Told You I Was Sick', while another nearby, erected by a man's widow, reads 'At least I know where he's sleeping tonight.'

The cemetery covers 21 acres (8.4 hectares) in the heart of Old Town, and many of the old stone caskets rest on the ground because the rock was too hard to dig for graves.

The Keys' proximity to Cuba is also brought home by the grave of the first missionary to Cuba who died at the age of 22. His tombstone bears the epitaph 'Don't Give Up the Cuban Mission'.

Close by lie the bodies of sailors who died when the US battleship *Maine* was sunk in Havana Harbor in 1898. The sinking sparked off the Spanish-American War.

There are also many tombstones carrying nicknames, such as Bunny, Shorty, The Tailor, Mamie, Lito and so on. The cemetery was relocated here from close to Southernmost Point after a devastating hurricane in 1846.

What has to be one of the most unusual crypts belongs to Jose J. Abreu, who was born on Key West and who was, at the time of going to press, still very much alive. The crypt carries all the nicknames by which he has been known such as Mr Clean, Baldy, Diablo, Uncle Tio, Primo, Nuts and many more. It also carries the inscription: 'The Buck Stops Here', and 'Call Me For Dinner'.

The cemetery is open daily from sunrise to dusk, and guided tours are available on Tuesday and Wednesday at 9am and 11am. There is a small charge for the tours which begin at the main entrance on Margaret Street.

KEY WEST CHARTER BOAT ROW

☎ 292-8167

35 deep-sea, light tackle and inshore boats for hire.

KEY WEST CIGAR FACTORY

3 Pirate's Alley
Off Mallory Square
☎ 294-3470

Watch cigars being made in the traditional hand-rolled way in the last surviving cigar factory on the island. Open daily.

KEY WEST FRAGRANCE AND ALOE

524 Front Street ☎ 294-5592

More than 300 fragrances and aloe products are made here and developed at the adjoining laboratory. Aloe is a very good treatment for sunburn. There is also a wide range of unusual and exotic scents and fragrances, including some featuring ginger and other tropical plants. Open from 9am to 5pm.

KEY WEST HANDPRINT

☎ 294-9535

Old Town fashion house with free guided tours and fashion shows to see how the fabrics are designed and made, and an opportunity to buy. Open daily.

KEY WEST LIGHTHOUSE AND MILITARY MUSEUM

938 Whitehead Street
☎ 294-0012

Opposite Hemingway House, this is Florida's third oldest brick lighthouse, built in 1847. The 90ft (27m) tall lighthouse houses the museum, which has exhibits about the history of Key West and the Keys, and memorabilia from the US battleship *Maine*, which was sunk in Havana Harbour, triggering the American Spanish War.

You can visit the lighthouse keeper's quarters and climb the 88-steps to the top of the lighthouse for great views over the city. Open daily 9.30am to 5pm. Admission charge.

KEY WEST SEAPLANE SERVICE

5603 College Road
☎ 296-6978

Sightseeing, snorkelling, adventure flights, birdwatching tours and overnight camping trips to Dry Tortugas National Park.

KEY WEST SHIPWRECK HISTOREUM

Mallory Square ☎ 292-8990

One of the city's latest attractions, and housed in wrecker Asa Tift's 1856 warehouse. It uses costumed actors, laser and other high-technology, as well as exhibits to tell the story of the wrecking era on Key West. Exhibits include items recovered from the *Isaac Allerton* which went down in August, 1865, carrying the richest manifest of any ship of its time.

There is also a 65ft (20m) observation tower which offers spectacular views over the Old Town and surrounding waters. Open for shows from 9.30am.

LANDS END VILLAGE

☎ 294-7491

A charming village and a mix of old-world charm and everything that Key West is today. There is the marina, with its fishing boats and charter fleet, which is a popular gathering place in the late afternoon as the boats return home with their catches. This contrasts with the delightful old shops, boutiques and restaurants.

Continued on p.92...

THE DRY TORTGAS

Fort Jefferson National Monument on Garden Key in the Dry Tortugas, is 70 miles (113km) west of Key West.

The Dry Tortugas were discovered by Ponce de Leon in 1513. They were named after the many turtles on the beach, and they were called dry, because there was no fresh water.

For centuries, the waters were a haven for pirates who could elude capture by hiding among the islands. Military analysts argued that whoever controlled the Dry Tortugas, a chain of seven coral reefs, would control shipping in the Gulf of Mexico.

The massive nineteenth-century dry-moated fort was started in 1846 and took 30 years to build. It never saw action, and was never actually completed. The fort was armed with 130 cannon and its three gun tiers could accommodate up to 450 cannon. Constructed to protect the southern flanks of the United States, it is still one of the largest coastal forts ever built anywhere in the United States.

Stonemasons were brought in from Germany and Ireland and, assisted by slaves, they laid millions of bricks shipped in from Virginia and Florida. Granite and slate was brought in from New England.

Although the walls are 8ft (2.4 m) thick and 50ft (15m) high, and despite its massive size, the fort has very shaky foundations. The military planners thought they were building it on rock, and did not realise that it was built on sand and coral boulders, which were prone to shifting. Within a few years, cracks had started to appear in the walls.

During the Civil War it was used as a Union prisoner-of-war camp, and Dr Samuel Mudd was imprisoned here for two years.

Dr Mudd was the Maryland physician who unwittingly set the broken leg of John Wilkes Booth, President Abraham Lincoln's assassin.

As a result, he was charged with being one of the 'Lincoln Conspirators', and sentenced to life imprisonment for complicity in the murder. Three other conspirators were also jailed for life and sent to the Fort, but what happened to them is unknown.

His unpopular action gave rise to the everyday expression, 'your name will be mud'. Later, the unfortunate doctor distinguished himself again and obtained a pardon, after selflessly helping fight a yellow fever epidemic in the garrison in 1867.

In 1874, the army abandoned the fort following a hurricane, but the Navy used it as a wireless station in the early 1900s and as a seaplane base in World War I. In 1935 it was declared a national monument by President Franklin D. Roosevelt.

Lighthouses were built on Garden Key in 1825 and on Loggerhead Key in 1856.

Apart from tours of the fort, including Mudd's cell, there are opportunities for snorkelling and sport fishing. The national monument now plays host to many rare migratory birds and the offshore waters are rich in marine life. On land you can see sooty and noddy terns, and at sea, there are four species of turtle including the endangered loggerhead turtles, French angelfish and many species of coral.

Camping is allowed in designated areas. There are rest rooms, but drinking water and all other supplies must be taken in.

Key West Seaplane Service has twice daily trips to Dry Tortugas from Murray's Marina on Stock Island, and reservations are recommended ☎ 294-7009.

Charter boats also make regular journeys to the monument.

THE KEY WEST WRITER'S WALK

☎ 294-1574

A conducted one-hour tour of the homes of many of the island's most famous literary sons and daughters.

THE LITTLE WHITE HOUSE MUSEUM

Front Street

Built in the 1890s, the house sprawls across a 2.2 acre (0.8 hectare) estate, and was the summer home of President Harry S. Truman during the late 1940s.

After his first visit in November 1946, he returned regularly every few months during his Presidency, and once wrote in a letter to his wife Bess, 'I've a notion to move the capital to Key West and just stay.' Open daily from 9am to 5pm.

MALLORY MARKET

On the waterfront

The market is an interesting shopping area where you can buy everything from the latest fashions to island arts and crafts.

Moreover, one cannot visit Key West without witnessing at least one spectacular sunset from this great vantage point. The place comes alive as the sun goes down with street artists, musicians and jugglers out in force to entertain the hundreds (and sometimes thousands) of people who gather for this nightly **Sunset Celebration** ritual.

Get there some time before sundown, and find a good position so that you can see the fantastic display as the huge red fireball that is the sun gently drops below the horizon, bathing the sky and sea in vividly changing colours. The sunset is always good, but when it is exceptional, the watchers show their appreciation by clapping.

MARRIOTT CASA MARINA RESORT

1500 Reynolds Street
☎ 296-3535 or
1-800-228-9290

This historic landmark building was originally built by Henry Flagler as the Key West terminus of the Overseas Railroad. Built in Spanish Renaissance-style, it is one of Key West's architectural gems. It is now a luxury hotel.

THE MEL FISHER MARITIME HERITAGE SOCIETY'S TREASURE MUSEUM

Greene Street
☎ 294-2633

Founded by the world's most successful treasure seeker!

Mel Fisher is a son of Key West, and has discovered many old wrecks, including the treasure-laden Spanish galleons, the *Santa Margarita* and the *Nuestra Señora de Atocha*, which foundered on reefs 45 miles (72km) west of Key West in 1622.

To date, he has recovered more than $400 million in gold and silver from the *Atocha* alone, which was found after a sixteen-year search. Many artifacts, weapons and some of the treasures, including gold, silver and jewelry from the wrecks, are on display. There is also a fascinating film about how sunken ships are located and their treasures recovered. Open daily from 10am to 5pm. Admission charge.

NANCY FORRESTER'S SECRET GARDEN

One, Free School Lane, opposite Heron House
☎ **294-0015**
Key West's own 'tropical rainforest': a world-class collection of tropical plants, many of them rare. Open daily 10am to 5pm.

NAUTILUS CRUISES

William Street
☎ **294-5266**
Based in Old Town, the company offers underwater cruises aboard a 92ft (28m) long surface 'submarine' with glass bottom, over the nearby reefs. Cruises daily.

NORTH AMERICAN RACING GREYHOUND TRACK

Fifth Avenue, Stock Island
☎ **294-9517**
The track has racing between November and April.

OLD CITY HALL

512 Greene Street
☎ **292-6718**
Built with its clock tower at the beginning of the twentieth century, to replace a wooden building which burned down in the 1866 fire.

The building has been restored to its former grandeur by the Historic Florida Keys Preservation Board. Open daily. The new City Hall is on Angela Street.

OLD TOWN TROLLEY

☎ **296-6688**
Offers sedate 90-minute tours of Key West. The all-weather trams have carved wooden seats, polished interiors and replica bells similar to those on the old-time San Francisco cable cars. The tours start and return in Mallory Square where you can park your own vehicle. The tour ticket allows you to get off at any of the fourteen stops en route to explore, and then board a later trolley. Daily tours leave every 30 minutes from 9am to 4.30pm.

PAN AMERICAN BUILDING

Caroline Street ☎ 293-8484
Worth a visit because it was the headquarters of Aero Marine Airways when they started flying mail and passenger services between Key West and Havana in the early 1920s.

Each flight carried a passenger homing pigeon, which could be released if the plane had to ditch! The birds were kept in the **Pigeon House**.

When the airline went out of business in 1924, it was taken over by Pan Am, and was the first international airport to be recognised by the US Post Office and allowed to carry air mail overseas. It is also home of Kelly's Caribbean Bar, Grill and Brewery, the island's only brewery.

PERKINS AND SON CHANDLERY

Fleming Street
☎ 294-7635
A unique collection 'salvaged' from wrecked ships and former Captains' homes in Old Town. Open daily.

PIER HOUSE INN AND RESORT

A luxury waterfront resort with private beach and a galaxy of first class restaurants. Even if you are not staying at the hotel, it is worth treating yourself to a meal or at least a cocktail on the Sunset Deck, to watch the sun go down.

RED BARN THEATRE

☎ 296-9911
Offers season productions of original dramas as well as musicals and contemporary classics.

RIPLEY'S BELIEVE IT OR NOT! MUSEUM

☎ 293-9896
Situated in the Strand Theatre and featuring the bizarre and unusual, collected by adventurer Robert Ripley over forty years. Exhibits range from shrunken heads and torture chambers to the mysteries of the ocean depths and incredible displays of craftsmanship from around the world. Open daily 10am to 11pm.

SAN CARLOS INSTITUTE

☎ 294-3887
This elegant Old Town building houses the centre for Cuban American studies, and traces its contribution to US history in films, lectures and exhibits. Open daily.

SLOPPY JOE'S BAR

☎ 294-5717
A must for all Hemingway fans. This is where the author enjoyed the occasional drink or four, and swapped stories with the other locals. It is very popular with live music into the early hours.

Continued on p.98...

Above: The most southerly point of the USA

Right: Conch Republic sign, Key West Airport

Below: Higgs Beach

SALT WATER FISHING CALENDAR FOR THE FLORIDA KEYS

Month	Species (catch limits apply to all species)	Best locations
Jan	trout bonefish, mangrove snapper sailfish, king and Spanish mackerel	Upper Keys all waters offshore trolling
Feb	tarpon trout, redfish cero, king mackerel	near bridges, channels Florida Bay No Man's Land, south of the Dry Tortugas
March	trout, snook bonefish sailfish, king and Spanish mackerel snapper, grouper	Florida Bay, inshore bridges flats offshore reefs & flats south of the Dry Tortugas
April	trout, snook bonefish tarpon sailfish	Upper Keys, Florida Bay flats channels & near bridges trolling offshore
May	tarpon trout, snook bonefish sailfish grouper and snapper	passes, under bridges Upper Keys flats, Upper & Middle Keys offshore south east of Key West
June	trout, redfish tarpon, mangrove snapper bone fish sailfish snapper, grouper	Upper Keys all areas flats, Upper & Middle Keys trolling offshore reefs between Marathon & Islamorada

SALT WATER FISHING CALENDAR FOR THE FLORIDA KEYS

July	King mackerel, barracuda, bonito,	Coffin's Patch between Islamorada & Marathon
	sailfish	
	redfish (July to December)	Florida Bay
August	bonefish	flats
	trout, redfish	channels
	grouper, yellowtail, mangrove & mutton snapper	offshore reefs
Sept	bonefish	flats
	grouper, snapper	reefs
	tarpon	channels
	dolphin	Gulf Stream
	trout, redfish, snook	Florida Bay
Oct	pompano, sailfish, wahoo, tuna, dolphin, king mackerel, bonito	Gulf Stream
	bluefish	inshore
	cobia	from bridges
	trout, redfish	channels
Nov	pompano, blackfin tuna, barracuda, bonito, dolphin, sailfish, wahoo	Gulf Stream
	bonefish	flats
	trout, snook, redfish	Florida Bay
	grouper, amberjack	reefs
Dec	pompano, sailfish, wahoo, amberjack, barracuda, blackfin tuna, little tunny, dolphin, grouper, king mackerel	offshore
	bonefish	inshore, sand flats
	cobia, grouper	reefs, near bridges
	snook, redfish	backcountry
	trout	bayside grass

SMATHERS BEACH

Has picnic tables, jet ski rentals and is popular as a parasailing area.

SOLARIS HILL

Worth climbing just to say you have scaled the city's highest point – 16ft (5m) above sea level.

SOUTHERNMOST POINT

The Southernmost Point in the United States is marked by a much photographed, land-locked large red striped buoy.

Standing at the corner of Whitehead and South Streets, you are only 90 miles (145km) from Cuba and 150 miles (242km) from Miami. There is very short term parking to allow you to get your photographs.

ST PAUL'S EPISCOPAL CHURCH

Corner of Duval and Eaton Streets ☎ 296-5142
Three churches on the site have been destroyed by storms and hurricanes and the present structure dates from 1919. Open daily.

TENNESSEE WILLIAMS FINE ARTS CENTER

Florida Keys Community College ☎ 296-1520
The centre, dedicated to the writer and playwright who spent a lot of his life in the Keys, stages theatre, dance, concert and films.

THOMAS RIGGS WILDLIFE REFUGE

South Roosevelt Boulevard ☎ 294-2116
A great place for birdwatching with platform vantage points. Open daily.

TURTLE KRAALS MUSEUM

200 Margaret Street ☎ 294-0209
Learn about turtles and the perils they face.
Lands End Village ☎ 294-2640
A marine turtle exhibit with endangered loggerhead turtles and many other marine species in the large holding tanks. You can also see shark, stingray, tropical fish and giant crawfish.

There are also hospital tanks where injured 'patients' are recovering, and a touch tank. Although part of a restaurant complex, none of the exhibits is destined for the menu! Open Monday to Saturday 11am to 10.30pm, Sunday 12noon to 10.30pm. Admission free.

THE WATERFRONT PLAYHOUSE

Mallory Square ☎ 294-5015
Stages season productions of original dramas, musicals and contemporary classics.

WRECKER'S MUSEUM

322 Duval Street ☎ 294-9502
The oldest house on Key West, dating from 1829, although a slightly later neighbouring

property was connected to it in the 1840s.

It exhibits ship models, antiques and a fascinating collection of miniature Conch houses, as well as describing the history and life of the wreckers.

It is named after Francis B.Watlington, a sea captain turned wrecker. Open daily from 10am to 4pm. Admission charge.

KEY WEST FESTIVALS

Key West enjoys a number of festivals during the year. These include **Old Island Days**, which commemorates the island's history, heritage and traditions. It starts in December and continues for four months. Houses and gardens are tidied up, and floodlights illuminate the most attractive properties which are thrown open to the public for guided tours.

Another part of the Old Island Days festivities is the Conch Shell-blowing Competition. During the days of the wreckers, the conch shell was used like a trumpet to alert people that a ship had gone aground on the reefs.

The **Conch Republic Independence Celebrations** take place in April, and commemorate the 'tongue in cheek' declaration of independence on 23 April, 1982.

Hemingway's birthday on 21 July is celebrated with the seven-day **Hemingway Days Festival**, which includes the Hemingway look-alike competition, short story contest, writer's workshop, storytelling competition and radio trivia quiz.

Fantasy Fest takes place over ten days in late October and welcomes in the fall/winter season. It is a cross between Halloween, Mardi Gras and Carnival, and is centred on Old Town. There are food fests, children's day, concerts, arts and crafts shows, costume competitions and parades, and culminating in the Saturday night Twilight Fantasy Parade of floats.

NIGHTSPOTS

The Copa
623 Duval Street ☎ 296-8521
For the zany and outrageous.

Captain Tony's Saloon
428 Greene Street ☎ 294-1838
Good for a drink and celebrity spotting — the place to go to see and be seen.

Sloppy Joe's
201 Duval Street ☎ 294-5717
Made famous by Hemingway, and always lively.

Other lively spots include: **Origami**, Duval Square ☎ 294-0092, **Marro City**, Duval Street ☎ 293-0039, **Two Friends Patio Restaurant** and **Turtle Kraal Bar**.

EATING OUT ON KEY WEST

A&B Lobster House $$
Seafood
700 Front Street ☎ 294-5880
Casual no-nonsense eating place
where the food is everything.
Open Monday to Saturday 11am
to 9pm.

Bahama Mama's Kitchen $$
Bahamian Cuisine
Corner of Whitehead & Petronia
☎ 294-3355
Lively dining and great seafood,
especially the
conch dishes.

Benihana $$
Steaks & seafood
S.Roosevelt Blvd (next to Martha's)
☎ 294-6400
Great steak, shrimp, lobster and
chicken prepared
by your own personal chef. Open
for dinner.

Blond Giraffe $-$$
Coffee bar and bakery
629 Duval Street ☎ 293-6667
Enjoy the best Key Lime Pie in Key
West.
Open 9am - 11pm.

Cafe Marquesa $$-$$$
American
Marquesa Hotel, Fleming St
☎ 292-1919
American, great food and
deservedly popular. Open daily for
dinner.

Camille's $$
Exotic American
1202 Simonton Street ☎ 296-4811
Recently relocated to cope with
growing demand, this all-day
eatery offers great food in a fun
atmosphere.

Captain Runaground Harvey's $$
Upmarket Pub Grub
Garrison Bight Marina
☎ 305-296-9907
Floating Pub that is very popular
with the locals - always a good
sign. Good food, great value.

Cole's Peace $-$$
Bakery cafe
930 Eaton street ☎ 292-6511
Great breads, sandwiches and
soups. Try the herbal teas.

Duval Beach Club $$
American and seafood
1405 Duval Street ☎ 295-6550
Fun dining on the beach

Half Shell Raw Bar $$
Fish and seafood
231 Margaret Street ☎ 294-7496
Quayside dining in this traditional
Key West fish house.

Iguana Cafe $
American
425 Green Street ☎ 296-6420
Open all day.

Jimmy Buffet's Margaritaville $$
American-Caribbean
500 Duval Street ☎ 292-1435
An institution!! Great food and
entertainment.

Kelly's Caribbean Bar and Grill $$
Island cuisine
303 Whitehead Street ☎ 293-7897
Relaxed dining, home-brewed beers.

Kyushu $-$$
American-Japanese
921 Truman Avenue ☎ 294-2995
Open for dinner.

La Trattoria Venezia $$
Italian-French
524 Duval Street ☎ 296-1075
Open for dinner. Reservations recommended.

Little Palm Island $$-$$$
Floridian- Caribbean
28500 Overseas Hwy, Little Torch Key
☎ 872-2524
Exquisite dining. Worth every penny!

Mangoes $-$$
Caribbean
700 Duval Street
☎ 292-4606
Open all day.

Martha's $$
Steak and seafood
S.Roosevelt Blvd ☎ 294-3466
Oceanfront dining with great food.

Meteor $$
Smokehouse
404 Southard Street ☎ 294-5602
Mouthwatering hickory-smoked pork, chicken, beef and fish.

Pier House Harbor View $$-$$$
Award-winning American
1 Duval Street ☎ 296-4600
Open all day.

Schooners Wharf Bar $$
Island cuisine and seafood
202 William Street ☎ 292-9520
Fun, lively waterside dining.

Shula's On the Beach
Steak and seafood
1435 Simonton Street ☎ 296-6144
Great food in fantastic oceanside setting.

Sloppy Joe's $$
A MUST Key West institution
201 Duval Street ☎ 294-5717

Square One $$-$$$
American and seafood
1075 Duval Street ☎ 296-4300
Excellent American cuisine, great wine list, lovely setting.

Sunset Pier Bar & Grill $$-$$$
Key West & American
Zero Duval Street ☎ 296-7701
Now open all day but perfect for sunset dinners.

Turtle Kraals Waterfront
Bar & Grill $$
Southwestern cooking and seafood
1 Lands End Village ☎ 294-2640
Lively waterfront dining, succulent food and great entertainment.

BEFORE YOU GO *

All visitors to the USA must have a valid passport with at least six months to run from the day they are scheduled to return home.

VISAS

Under the Visa Waiver Program, visitors from the UK, most EC countries and Japan, arriving by air or sea aboard a carrier participating in the programme, do not require a visa provided they do not plan to stay for more than 90 days. If travelling under this programme, you must complete a **green 'visa waiver form'**, which is handed to you at check-in, and which you hand in to the immigration officer to-gether with your passport.

Visitors with a valid visa must complete the white visa form.

Visitors making frequent trips to the USA or planning to stay for more than three months, should have a valid visa. Visa application forms can be obtained from Embassies and some travel companies and must be posted, together with your passport, photographs, and any other documents, to the visa section of the United States Embassy in your country. Allow at least 21 days for processing, although the visa is often returned earlier than this. Some travel companies offer fast track visa services in conjunction with the Embassy.

The normal tourist visa allows multiple entries to the US and is now valid for ten years. Visas granted some time ago, which were valid indefinitely, are now being cancelled by US Immigration officers as you enter the USA, so that you have to re-apply for the new 10-year visa, or switch to 'visa waiver' entry.

IMMIGRATION

Immigration procedures have been improved at most entry airports, but delays can be lengthy if, for instance, two Jumbo jets arrive within a few minutes of each other.

On arrival in the immigration hall you will be allocated to a queue and you must stay behind the line marked on the floor until called by the immigration officer. You may be asked to show your return air ticket to prove you plan to leave. Your passport will then be stamped with a date by which you must leave the country. A portion of the immigration form is stapled to your passport, and this has to be surrendered when leaving the country, so do not lose it.

Note: Immigration officers now insist that white visa and green visa-waiver forms are filled in correctly, and have the power to impose fines, rarely used, if not. Make sure your forms are filled in correctly, and if you make a mistake, get another from the cabin crew and fill it in again before submitting it to the immigration officer.

CUSTOMS

There are strict Customs and Department of Agriculture regulations governing what can and cannot be imported into the United States.

Needless to say, drugs, dangerous substances, firearms and ammunition are banned, as are a wide range of foods, such as meat, dairy products, fruit and vegetables in order to maintain the disease-free status of Florida's agriculture.

Florida has rabies, and pets being brought into the State either from abroad or elsewhere in the USA, should be vaccinated against the disease before arrival.

While there are no restrictions on how much cash you can take into the USA, all amounts over $10,000 must be listed on your customs declaration form. This is part of the authorities' fight against drug trafficking.

All gifts taken into the country and their value, should also be listed on the customs declaration, and should not be wrapped so that they are available for inspection if required. Duty is not payable if the total value of gifts and goods is under $400.

You are allowed to import duty-free into the USA, 200 cigarettes or 50 cigars or 2kg of tobacco, or proportionate amounts of each; 1 litre of alcoholic drinks (if aged 21 or over). If arriving by air from outside the USA, you will have to hand in your customs declaration after clearing immigration and picking up your checked-in luggage.

You can buy duty-free goods at the airport before departure, but you cannot pick up your purchases until just before you board the plane. After paying for your goods, you will be given a receipt, and you must remember to collect your goods from the duty-free staff who will be somewhere in the tunnel between the exit gate and plane.

ACCOMMODATION

HOTELS AND MOTELS

There is a huge range of hotel and motel accommodation to choose from as you travel through the Keys. Categories range from luxury to basic, and there is something to suit all tastes and pockets.

Modern hotels and motels usually offer two double beds in each room and, as you pay for the room, this can work out very reasonably if you are travelling with family or close friends.

Rooms usually have en suite bathroom and telephone, air-conditioning and cable/satellite television as standard. Older rooms tend to be smaller and often have just a single or double bed.

Because competition is intense, prices are generally lower than comparable accommodation elsewhere, even in the high season, and there are usually added incentives to tempt you. These can range from free breakfasts to free watersports and boat trips.

Prices vary according to season and standards of service offered. Most hotel chains offer vouchers which if pre-paid offer substantial discounts so it is worth checking with your travel company. Before buying vouchers, however, make sure the hotel offers the standard of service you require.

There are also substantial discounts for senior citizens, and members of the American Automobile Association, which may be worth joining even if you do not live in the United States but make frequent trips to it.

If visiting during the peak season, between Christmas and May, it is advisable to reserve accommodation. At other times, you may want to cruise around, and hunt out the best bargains. All motels and hotels clearly advertise their prices and any perks on offer, and you can always pop in and check out the room before deciding. If you feel up to it, you can always haggle over the price and see if you can get a few dollars knocked off for staying several nights, paying cash or whatever. Nothing ventured, nothing gained.

Many hotels and large motels have their own restaurants, and will usually offer American Plan (AP) equivalent to full board ie accommodation and all meals, or Modified Plan (MP) which offers accommodation plus breakfast and dinner. If the establishment has no restaurant, there is usually coffee available in the lobby, and free doughnuts are often available in lieu of breakfast. Ice machines and soft drinks vending machines are generally available.

For Overseas Visitors

Rooms are also much larger than in Europe, and can often accommodate an extra single bed or cot, which will be provided for a small additional fee provided adequate notice is given.

CONDOMINIUMS

A condominium or condo is an apartment of several rooms. There may be just a few condos in the building or hundreds in a high-rise block. Many people from out-of-state buy condos as an investment, and a place for their summer holidays, and rent them out through agents when they are not there. They can be available for rent from a week to long lets. They offer more space and privacy than a hotel or motel room, and for larger groups, work out much cheaper.

RESORTS

These usually consist of a large hotel built in its own grounds, usually on the beach, and offering first-class accommodation, food, entertainment and a wide range of facilities which may include land and water-based sports, boat cruises, sea fishing and dive center.

BED AND BREAKFAST/GUESTHOUSES

Worth hunting out if you want a taste of real Florida living. They are often more expensive than a cheap motel or hotel, but they do allow you to stay in a family home. Local tourist offices have lists of homes offering bed and breakfast accommodation, and guest houses, also known as boarding houses.

Above: Tiki Bars are found throughout the Keys

Below: Islamorada Visitor Center

*Opposite: All the Keys are excellent for snorkelling.
This was taken at Marathon*

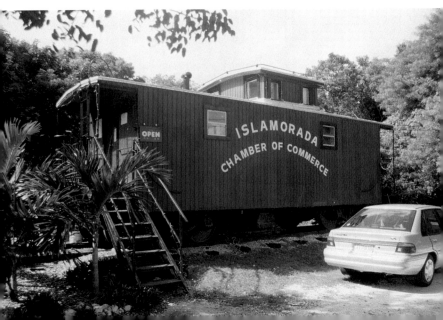

Fact File

* For
Overseas
Visitors

RENTAL HOMES

There are many private homes available for rental on the Keys. The standard of property varies enormously. Most homes are furnished to high standards, have air-conditioning and many have their own swimming pools. Many also come with housekeeping services. For larger families and groups, the cost of renting a three or four bedroom house, or even two near each other, is significantly cheaper than comparable hotel accommodations.

*Accommodation is generally listed as oceanside, bayside or gulfside, that is on the Atlantic Ocean, Florida Bay or the Gulf of Mexico.

KEY LARGO TO ISLAMORADA

Amy Slate's Amoray Dive Resort $-$$ (MM 104)
104250 Overseas Highway
Key Largo
☎ 451-3595 or
1-800-426-6729
Bayside apartments with scuba, snorkelling and boat trips.

Anchorage Resort and Yacht Club $$ (MM 107.5)
107500 Overseas Highway
Key Largo
☎ 451-0500
Small, comfortable waterfront resort with heated pool, jacuzzi, tennis, shuffleboard, deck fishing, pier, marina, gift shop.

Bay Harbor Lodge $
(MM 97.5)
97702 Overseas Highway
Key Largo
☎ 852-5695
A small friendly lodge in tropical gardens on the bay.

With boat dock, ramp and free use of boats, or laze in one of the hammocks strung between trees in the garden. Good value.

Bayside Resort $
(MM 99.5)
99490 Overseas Highway
Key Largo
☎ 451-4450
Small, comfortable bayside resort with tropical landscaping and palm fringed beach. Rooms have kitchens and there are boat docks.

Best Western Suites, Key Largo $-$$ (MM 100)
201 Ocean Drive, Key Largo
☎ 451-5081
Well equipped town house suites with kitchen and 2 baths, pool, large dock, snorkelling and diving. Good value.

Fact File

Coconut Palm Inn $-$$
(MM 92)
198 Harborview Drive,
Tavernier
☎ 852-3017
Comfortable bayside accommodation, with pool, marina, boat dock and ramp, screened decks, diving training.

Divers Cove $ (MM 95.5)
PO Box 583, Key Largo
☎ 852-5312
Small oceanside accommodation with marina, boat dock and ramp, snorkelling, fishing, free canoe and paddleboat.

Gilbert's Resort
$-$$ (MM 107.5)
107900 Overseas Highway, at Jewfish Creek in Key Largo
☎ 451-1133 or
1-800-457-1233
Right on the waterfront, with boat ramp, small restaurant and bar and nearby marina. Music and dancing Friday and Saturday.

Howard Johnson Resort
$$ (MM 102)
On US1, Key Largo
☎ 451-1400 or
1-800-947-7320
On Florida Bay, with restaurant, bar, pool, private beach, gift shops, sailing and watersports. Nightly entertainment.

Hungry Pelican Motel $
(MM 99.5)
PO Box 762, Key Largo
☎ 451-3576
Peaceful bayside motel with boat docks and ramp, free canoes, water sports rentals and sandy beach.

Jules Undersea Lodge
$$-$$$ (MM 103.2)
51 Shoreland Drive,
Key Largo
☎ 451-2353 or
1-800-22-OCEAN
A fascinating resort which offers the chance to sleep underwater in one of two submarine suites which come complete with large observation portholes, living room, entertainment centre, stocked refrigerator, kitchen and round the clock room service. Guests must have diving experience, or complete a three hour basic course at the Lodge before being allowed to stay overnight.

Key Largo Inn $$ (MM 99)
PO Box 2843, Key Largo
☎ 451-2478
Oceanside inn with 50 comfortable rooms, pool and tennis.

Fact File

* For
Overseas
Visitors

Largo Lodge $$ (MM 101.5)
101740 Overseas Highway
Key Largo
☎ 451-0424, or
1-800-IN-THE-SUN
Small, adults-only bayside
property in tropical gardens,
with fishing and diving, boat
dock and ramp.

**Marina Del Mar Resort and
Marina** $$-$$$ (MM 100)
527 Caribbean Drive,
Key Largo
☎ 451-4107 or
1-800-451-3483
Offers restaurant, bar, large
pool, tennis, fitness centre,
deepwater marina, diving,
snorkelling, fishing, boat
cruises and sailing.

**Marriott's Key Largo Bay
Beach Resort** $$-$$$
103800 Overseas Highway,
Key Largo
☎ 453-0000 or
1-800-932-9332
New luxury bayfront resort
with restaurant, bars, live
entertainment nightly, pool,
private beach, dive shop,
marina, gift shop and confer-
ence facilities.

Neptune's Hideaway
$-$$ (MM 104.2)
104180 Overseas Highway,
Key Largo
☎ 451-0357
By a sandy beach with free
paddleboats, canoes and
bicycles, and boat dock.

Ocean Pointe Suites $$
(MM 92.5)
500 Burton Drive, Tavernier
☎ 853-3000 or
1-800-882-9464
Large oceanfront property
with large pool, sandy
beach, cafe, lounge, tennis,
dive center, marina, boat
deck and ramp.

Popp's Motel $-$$
(MM 95.5)
95500 Overseas Highway
Key Largo
☎ 852-5201
A small, popular bayside
resort with cottages close to
sandy beach, hot tub,
watersports, barbecue, boat
dock and ramp. Great for
watching dolphins, manatees
and waterbirds. Good value.

Ramado Resort $$
99751 Overseas Highway
☎ 451-3939
Very comfortable 90 room
bayside resort with pool,
barbecue, bar, restaurant,
watersports and 75 slip
marina.

Sea Trail Motel $ (MM 98.6)
Route 5 Box 91, Key Largo
☎ 852-8001
Good value budget bayside
accommodation.

Seafarer Fish and Dive Resort

$ (MM 97.8)
PO Box 185, Key Largo
☎ 852-5349
Very comfortable bayside resort in lush, tropical gardens, with sandy beach, jacuzzi, barbecues, boat dock and ramp, free paddle, row and sail boats, kayaks, fishing, dive centre and snorkelling, boat and dive trips. Good value.

Sheraton Beach Resort

$$-$$$
97000 South Overseas Highway, Key Largo
☎ 852-5553 or
1-800-826-1006
Large, luxury resort with 3 restaurants, bars, 2 pools, children's activity centre, tennis, island beach, watersports, nature trails and 21 slip marina.

Sunset Cove Beach Resort $
(MM 99.5)
PO Box 99, Key Largo
☎ 451-0705
Small bayside motel with boat dock and ramp, tropical gardens, free sail and paddle boats, canoes and windsurfers, and fishing pier.

Tavernier Hotel $
(MM 91.8)
91865 Overseas Highway
Tavernier
☎ 852-4131
Oceanside bed and breakfast hotel with two restaurants.

Vacation Homes And Condo Rental With Reservation Services

Accommodation Tan Keys
☎ 451-1013

Century 21 Keysearch Realty
☎ 451-4321

Coldwell Banker Keys Realty
☎ 852-5254

Condominium Moon Bay
call collect ☎ (813) 939-3612

Florida Bay Club
☎ 451-0101

Freelancer Limited
☎ 451-0349

Largolux Corp
☎ 448-2276

Loveland Realty Vacation Rentals
☎ 451-5055

MARR Properties
☎ 451-4078

Ocean Drive Apartments
☎ 221-6711

Paradise Connections
☎ 852-2405

Port Largo Condominium Association
☎ 451-4847

Port Largo Duplex
☎ 662-3922

Fact File

*Bed and Breakfast
Islamorada*

* For
Overseas
Visitors

Breezy Palms Resort $$

(MM 80)
PO Box 767
☎ 664-2361
Oceanside resort with pool
set in tropical gardens,
beach, boat dock and ramp,
snorkelling, and games.
Good value.

Caloosa Cove Resort

$$ (MM 73.8)
73801 Overseas Highway
☎ 664-8811
Oceanside resort with restau-
rant, lounge, tennis, marina,
boat dock and ramp.

Cheeca Lodge $$-$$$

(MM 82.5) Upper
Matecumbe
☎ 664-4651 or
1-800-327-2888
A large luxury resort which
attracts an impressive guest
list and offers a wide range
of amenities, including
nature trail, golf, parasailing,
fishing, tennis and dive
school, with excellent Atlan-
tic's Edge Restaurant and
Ocean Terrace Grill, bar,
large pools,1,000ft (305m)
beachfront and salt-water
lagoon. Camp Cheeca is
designed to educate children
aged 6 to 12 about the
fragile ecology of the Florida
Keys in a fun, learning envi-
ronment. Nightly entertain-
ment Monday to Saturday.
Extensive conference facili-
ties.

Chesapeake Resort $$-$$$

83409 Overseas Highway
☎ 664-4662 or
1-800-338-3395
A spacious oceanfront resort
set in 6 acres (2.5 hectares)
of tropical gardens, with
restaurant, bar, pools, tennis,
fishing, diving, snorkelling,
gym, lagoon and conference
facilities.

Days Inn $-$$ (MM 82.5)

82749 Overseas Highway
☎ 664-3681
Oceanview suites and villas
with pool, fishing pier and
boat dock.

Drop Anchor Resort Motel

$-$$ (MM 85)
PO Box 22
☎ 664-4863
Oceanside with pool, boat
dock and ramp.

Edgewater Lodge $

(MM 65.5)
PO Box 799
☎ 305-664-4418
Units right on the Bay-Dock,
small sandy beach.

Golden Key Motel $-$$

(MM 81.5)
PO Box 710 US1
☎ 664-4418
Quiet bayside motel rooms
and efficiencies in tropical

gardens, with sandy beach, boat basin, dock, ramp and fantastic views.

Harbor Lights Motel $$

84001 Overseas Highway
☎ 664-3611 or
1-800-327-7070
Waterside motel resort close to coral reefs and wrecks of Spanish galleons. Offers palm-shaded pool and watersports. Good value.

Hibiscus Resort $-$$

(MM 82)
PO Box 85
☎ 664-8787
Oceanside studios and apartments with boat dock and ramp.

Holiday Isle Beach Resorts

$$-$$$ (MM 84.5)
84001 Overseas Highway
☎ 664-2321 or
1-800-327-7070
The complex includes the Holiday Isle Beach Resort, Howard Johnson Resort at Holiday Isle and El Capitan Harbor Lights. The resort with Polynesian-touches, offers a variety of accommodation from luxury rooms to well-appointed apartments around the heated pool. There are five restaurants including the great value Horizon Restaurant with its lively bar, white sand beach, shops, marina, boat ramp, diving, watersports and

fishing. There is nightly enter-tainment in the lounge. The resort offers full conference facilities.

Islamorada Motel $

(MM 87.5)
87760 Overseas Highway
☎ 852-9376
Bayside motel with saltwater pool, fishing charters and dive packages. Good value.

Islander Resort $ (MM 82.1)

PO Box 766, ☎ 664-2031
Set in 20 acres (8 hectares) beside the ocean, with pool and fishing pier.

Kon Tiki Resort $$ (MM 81)

Route 1 Box 58
☎ 664-4702
Bayside with sandy beach, fishing, saltwater pool, boat dock and ramp.

La Jolla Resort $ (MM 82.3)

82216 Overseas Highway
☎ 664-9213
Bayside with beach, grills, games, boat dock and ramp.

La Siesta Resort $-$$

(MM 80)
PO Box 573
☎ 664-2132
Oceanside with pool and waterslide, playground, waverunner rentals, boat slips and fishing pier.

Above: Cheeca Lodge, Islamorada

Below: Happy moments at the Sheraton Suites, Key West

Opposite: The old and new Seven Mile Bridges

Fact File

* For Overseas Visitors

Lime Tree Bay Resort
$-$$ (MM 68.5)
PO Box 839
☎ 664-4740
Bayside with restaurant, pool, boat dock, boat rentals and tennis.

Moorings Village $$
(MM 81.5)
123 Beach Road
☎ 664-4708
Secluded oceanside units with beautiful beach, pool and tennis.

Ocean Dawn Lodge $
(MM 82.8)
82885 Old Highway
☎ 664-4844
Oceanside units with boat dock and ramp, boat rental, sports and close to amenities.

Pelican Cove Resort
$$-$$$ (MM 84.5)
84457 Old Overseas Highway
☎ 664-4435 or 1-800-445-4690
On its own beach with pool, poolside bar, watersports, tennis, sailing, windsurfing, scuba and fishing. Good value.

Pines and Palms Resort
$$-$$$
80401 Overseas Highway
☎ 664-4343
Cozy cottages set in tropical gardens beside the ocean. Pool and dock. Great value.

Ragged Edge Resort
$-$$ (MM 86.5)
243 Treasure Harbor
☎ 852-5389
Secluded and quiet small oceanfront property with pool, fishing pier, marina, boat dock and ramp, games and free bikes.

Sands of Islamorada $-$$
(MM 80)
80051 Overseas Highway
☎ 664-2791
Oceanfront with pool, hot tub, boat dock and ramp – and parrots.

Sea Isle Resort and Marina
$$ (MM 82)
109 E Carroll Street
☎ 664-2235
Oceanside with sandy beach, fishing pier, marina, boat dock and ramp.

Shoreline Motel $ (MM 81.5)
Route 1 Box 5
☎ 664-4077
Bayside with beach, boat dock and ramp.

Smugglers Cove Resort and Marina $-$$ (MM 85.5)
85500 Overseas Highway
☎ 664-5564
Bayside with restaurant, lounge, bait and tackle shop, boat and watersport rentals and dive shop.

Tropic Air Resort $
(MM 75.8)
75780 Overseas Highway
☎ 664-4989
Bayside with sandy beach
and deepwater protected
boat basin.

Tropical Reef Resort $$
(MM 85)
84977 Overseas Highway
☎ 664-8881
Oceanside with floating
breakfast cafe, pool, beach,
basketball, jacuzzi, marina,
boat dock and ramp.

White Court Gate $$-$$$
76010 Overseas Highway
☎ 664-4136
Old charm, moden comfort
and exclusive. Seven units
set in large tropical gardens
close to the sea.

*Vacation homes and condo
rental with reservation
services*
**American Caribbean
Real Estate**
☎ 664-5152
Angler's Realty
☎ 664-9166
Best of Both Worlds
☎ 664-4475
Century 21 Coastways
☎ 664-4637
**Freewheeler Vacation
Realty**
☎ 664-2075
Futura Yacht Club
☎ 852-8816

Long Key Realty
☎ 664-9454
Palms of Islamorada Condo
☎ 664-8000
Paradise Connection
☎ 852-2405
Remax/Anchor Realty
☎ 664-4446
Tropical Diversion
☎ 474-9010

MARATHON TO
LOWER KEYS

**Banana Bay Resort and
Marina** $$-$$$ (MM 49.5)
4590 Overseas Highway
☎ 1-800-BANANA-1/
743-3500
A luxury bayside resort set in
10 acres (4 hectares), with
lovely spacious rooms,
restaurant, poolside lounge,
massive tropical pool, sandy
beach, and snorkelling area,
plus tennis, health and
fitness centre and nearby
golf. Charter boats are avail-
able for fishing, diving and
sailing. Conference facilities.

Bonefish Bay Motel $
(MM 53.5)
12565 Overseas Highway
Marathon, ☎ 289-0565
Oceanside with pool, boat
dock and ramp, Saturday
barbecues, games and card
room.

Fact File

* For Overseas Visitors

Bonefish Resort $
(MM 58.1)
Route 1 Box 343, Grassy Key
☎ 743-7107
Oceanside with free canoes, row and paddle boat and windsurfers.

Captain Pips Marina & Hideaway
$-$$ (MM 47.5)
1410 Overseas Highway
☎ 743-4403
Excellent budget accommo-dation. A great get-away place, ideal for boaters, anglers and tourists.

Coco Plum Beach and Tennis Club $$-$$$
(MM 54.5)
Coco Plum Drive
☎ 743-0240 or
1-800-228-1587
Oceanfront luxury villas with pool, tennis and watersports, and close to all amenities.

Coco Plum Beach Villas/ Royal Plum $$-$$$
(MM 54.8)
☎ 289-1102
Quiet, oceanfront with 200ft (61m) beach on undevel-oped island with pool and tennis.

Conch Key Cottages
$-$$ (MM 62.3)
Route 1 Box 424
☎ 289-1377
Oceanside cottages and apartments with pool, sun-beach, private island harbor, boat dock and ramp.

Continental Inn $$
1121 W. Ocean Drive
Marathon
☎ 289-0101
Affordable family resort with one and two bedroom condos by private beach and heated pool.

Coral Lagoon Resort
$ (MM 53.5)
12399 Overseas Highway
☎ 289-0121
Oceanside with pool and boat dock.

Duck Inn $-$$
(MM 61)
Route 1 Box 1128
☎ 289-7567
Oceanside with pool, pro-tected waterfront dock and boat ramp.

Fara Blanco Resort and Marina
$-$$ (MM 48)
1996 Overseas Highway, Marathon
☎ 743-9018
Resort with wide range of accommodation on both the Atlantic and the Gulf, includ-ing floating houseboat staterooms and lighthouse apartments, with restaurants, lounges, Olympic-size pool, full service marina, boat ramp, fishing and diving charters, boat rentals and shops.

Grassy Key Beach Motel
$ (MM 58.5)
Route 1 Box 357
☎ 743-0533
Oceanside with private sandy beach, row boats, canoes and boat dock.

Gulfview Resort
$ (MM 58.5)
Route 2 Box 543 Grassy Key
☎ 289-1414
Bayside in sheltered cove with heated pool, free fun boats, rental power boats, boat ramp and watersports.

Hawk's Cay Resort and Marina $$-$$$ (MM 61)
Duck Key
☎ 743-7000 or
1-800-432-2242
A lovely West Indian-style oceanside resort set on its own 60-acre (24-hectare) island with delightful accommodation. It has four restaurants including the very good Caribbean Room, and offers excellent buffet break-fast, pool, beach, protected lagoon and dolphin training facility, whirlpool spas, tennis, fishing, sailing, diving,watersports, cycling, fitness trail, games room and kiddies club. The marina has 60 yacht slips. It has extensive conference facilities.

Hidden Harbor Motel $
(MM 48.5)
2396 Overseas Highway
☎ 743-5376

A newly remodelled motel with rooms and efficiencies, and 700ft (213m) of waterfront, with pool, boat dock and ramp, snorkelling, fishing and charter boats. Close to all amenities and noted for its turtle hospital, founded by owner Richie Moretti, which also researches into a tumour causing disease that attacks and kills huge numbers of these sea creatures around the world.

Holiday Inn Resort & Marina
$$-$$$
13201 Overseas Highway, Marathon,
☎ 800-224-5053
134 Luxury rooms with ocean front pool, tiki bar, restaurant and lounge.

Key Colony Beach Botel
$-$$ (MM 54)
Box 24, Key Colony Beach
☎ 289-0821
Oceanside with pool, boat dock and ramp, and Club privileges.

Key Colony Point $$
(MM 53.9)
1133 W Ocean Drive, Key Colony Beach
☎ 743-7701
Oceanside spacious units all with seaviews, pool, tennis and beach.

Fact File

* For
Overseas
Visitors

Key Lime Resort $$
(MM 53)
11600 Ist Avenue Gulf
☎ 743-3505
Bayside with pool, bike
rentals, bait, tennis, volley-
ball and boat dock.

Kingsail Resort Motel $
(MM 50.5)
7050 Overseas Highway
☎ 743-5246 or
1-800-423-7474
A small resort built round the
pool and close to the fishing
boat dock, with grill, boat
ramps, dive shop, fishing
and boat charters, small
grocery shop.

Marathon Key Beach Club
$$ (MM 49.5)
4560 Overseas Highway,
Marathon
☎ 743-6522
Oceanside condos with all
amenities, pool, hot tub,
marina, boat ramp.

Ocean Beach Club $
(MM 53.5)
351 E Ocean Drive,
Key Colony Beach
☎ 289-0525
Oceanside with pool, jacuzzi,
beach, fishing pier and
games.

**Pelican Motel and
Trailer Park**
$ (MM 59)
Route 1 Box 528
☎ 289-0011
Bayside with pool, boat dock
and ramp, and 85 RV sites
with full hook-up.

Rainbow Bend Resort $$
(MM 58)
Route 1 Box 159
☎ 289-1505
Oceanside efficiencies with
full American breakfast, pool,
boat dock and some use of
resort's boats.

Reef Resort $-$$ (MM 50.5)
6800 Overseas Highway,
Marathon
☎ 743-7900
Bayside with pool, tennis,
clubhouse, games room,
paddle boats, canoes and
cycles, boat dock and ramp.

Sandlewood Lodge $
(MM 53.5)
PO Box 523148, Marathon
☎ 743-4922
Oceanside with boat dock,
boat rental, bait and tackle.

Sea Dell Motel $ (MM 49.8)
5000 Overseas Highway
☎ 743-5161
Bayside with rooms and
efficiencies and pool, and
close to all amenities.

Seahorse Motel and Marina
$ (MM 51)
7196 Overseas Highway,
Marathon,
☎ 743-6571
Pool, marina and boat ramp,
dive and fishing charters
available.

**Seascape Oceanfront
Resort** $ (MM 51)
E 76th Street
☎ 743-6455
Quiet, oceanfront units in

spacious grounds with tidal pool, boat dock and ramp, and fishing pier.

Seashell Beach Resort
$ (MM 57.5)
Route 1, Box 154
☎ 289-0265
Oceanside with sandy beach, boat dock and ramp, free row boats, 300ft (92m) long fishing pier, snorkel and live coral patch reef.

Seaward Resort Motel $
(MM 51.5)
8700 Overseas Highway, Marathon,
☎ 743-5711
Oceanside with large pool, tanning deck, fishing pier, boat dock and ramp.

Sombrero Resort $$
(MM 50)
19 Sombrero Boulevard, Marathon
☎ 1-800-433-8660
An all-suite resort with restaurant, lounge, beach bar, pool, sauna, floodlit tennis, marina and nearby golf. Conference facilities.

Tropical Cottages $
(MM 50)
243 61st Street, Marathon
☎ 743-6048
Bayside tropical cottages with spa, row boats, fishing, boat dock and ramp.

Valhalla Beach Resort $
(MM 56)
Route 2 Box 115
☎ 289-0616

Oceanside in lush gardens with private beach, boat dock and ramp.

Yellowtail Inn $$ (MM 62)
58162 Overseas Highway, Grassy Key
☎ 743-8400
Charming laid back property on the ocean.

Vacation homes and condo rental with reservation services

Brenner Realty
☎ 743-5000

Castillo Del Sol Condominiums
☎ 743-8313

Century 21-Heart of the Keys
☎ 743-3377

Coldwell Banker/Schmitt Realty
☎ 743-5181

Conch Realty Vacation Rentals
☎ 743-8877

DelCane Realty
☎ 743-0772

Dolphin Vacations
☎ 743-9876

East Sister Rock-Unique Island Vacations
☎ 289-1641

Florida Keys Escape
☎ (516) 878-6296

Florida Key Reservations
☎ 289-1104

Fact File

Fact File

*For Overseas Visitors

Key Colony Beach Realty
☎ 743-6226

Land and Sea Realty
☎ 743-6494

Sea Isle Condos
☎ 743-0173

Simone Tours
☎ 743-5274

Sunwater Vacation Rentals
☎ 743-0391

LOWER KEYS

**B and B on Ocean —
Casa Grande** $ (MM 33)
Box 378
☎ 872-2878
Quiet oceanside b&b, with beach, hot tub, snorkelling equipment, boat dock and ramp. Adults only.

Big Pine Resort Motel $
(MM 30.5)
Route 5 Box 796,
Big Pine Key
☎ 872-9090
Bayside efficiencies with restaurant, pool and boat parking.

Caribbean Village $$
(MM 11)
1211 Overseas Highway
☎ 296-9542
Bayside with boat ramp and dock space.

Deer Run Guesthouse
$-$$ (MM 33)
Box 431,
☎ 872-2015
Oceanside with beach, hot tub in cracker-style house

with huge verandah overlooking the water.

Dolphin Marina Resort $$
(MM 28.5)
Little Torch Key
☎ 872-2685 or
1-800-553-0308
Oceanside with well-equipped apartments, sun deck, live entertainment, rental powerboats, boat ramp, bait and tackle shop, equipment rental, daily snorkel cruises.

Little Palm Island $$$
Route 4, 1036
Little Torch Key
☎ 872-2524 or
1-800-GET LOST
The toll-free number says it all, a luxury get-away-from-it-all island resort just off Little Torch Key. Suites have their own whirlpool and bar, but no telephones and televisions are only available on request. There is a famed French restaurant, lounge, large lagoon pool with waterfall, sauna, sailing and a host of watersports. A place to be pampered.

**Looe Key Resort
& Dive Center** $$
Ramrod Key
☎ 872-2215
Features 5-star PADI dive center, restaurant, bar, pool and boat docks.

Top: There are many opportunities to explore the Keys by boat

Right: Gone fishing! Upper Matecumbe Key Marina

Below: Fishing is serious business in the Keys

123

Fact File

* For
Overseas
Visitors

**Old Wooden Bridge
Fishing Camp** $ (MM 30.5)
Route 5, Box 810,
Big Pine Key
☎ 872-2241
Bayside with bait shop,
marina, boat dock and ramp,
private bridge fishing.

Sugarloaf Lodge $-$$
(MM 17)
On US 1, Sugarloaf Key
☎ 745-3211
Accommodation is scattered
through the gardens which
overlook Sugarloaf Sound.
There is a waterside restaurant, tennis, miniature golf
and watersports.

*Vacation homes and
condo rental with
reservation services*

**Big Pine Key Vacation
Rentals**
☎ (708) 301-5397

Big Pine Vacation Rentals
☎ 872-9683

Brothers By The Bay
☎ 872-2449

Canal Cottage
☎ 872-3881

Century 21-Pro Realty
☎ 872-4148

**Coldwell Banker/Schmitt
Real Estate**
☎ 872-3050

ERA Lower Keys Realty
☎ 872-2258

Florida Keys Realty
☎ 743-3700

Greg O'Berry Inc
☎ 1-800-654-2781

Latitude 24 Real Estate
☎ 745-3425

Miley Real Estate
☎ 872-9403

Ocean Breeze House
☎ 1800-772-4560

**Outcast Charters and
Vacation Rentals**
☎ 1-800-833-9857

Raymond Real Estate
☎ 872-9116

REMAX Keys to the Keys
☎ 872-3399

Sugarloaf Realty
☎ 745-9082

Sullivan PA Inc
☎ 745-2777

**Waterfront Realty at
Venture Out RV Park**
☎ 745-1333

KEY WEST

Alexander Palms Court
$$-$$$
715 South Street
☎ 296-6413
Set in tropical gardens in Old
Town with pool and jacuzzi.

Almond Tree Inn $$
512 Truman Avenue
☎ 296-5415
Affordable accommodation
in the heart of the old town
close to the beach and
attractions.

Banana Bay Resort and Marina $-$$
2319 N Roosevelt Boulevard
☎ 296-6925
Luxury rooms by beach, with restaurant, pool, charter fishing, diving, sailing, watersports and shops.

Bananas Foster Bed and Breakfast $$
537 Caroline Street
☎ 294-9061
Lovely rooms in old town with hot tub and barbecue.

Best Western Key Ambassador Resort $-$$
3755 S. Roosevelt Boulevard
☎ 296-3500.
Modern oceanside hotel with pool, sundeck, continental breakfast, poolside lunch and close to beach.

Blue Lagoon $-$$
3101 N Roosevelt Boulevard
☎ 296-1043
Bayside with restaurant, bar, pool and watersports, boat dock and ramp.

Caribbean House Motel $
226 Petronia Street
☎ 296-1600
Caribbean-style property in Old Town close to all amenities.

Comfort Inn $-$$ (MM 2)
3824 N Roosevelt Boulevard
☎ 294-3773
Olympic size pool and free continental breakfast.

Cocunut Beach Resort $$$
1500 Alberta St
☎ 294-0057
Luxury resort and great getway for relaxing.

Courtyard $-$$$
910 Simonton Street
☎ 296-1148
Fully equipped suites in Old Town with pool, garden, private beach, gym membership.

Crowne Plaza La Concha Hotel $$-$$$
430 Duval Street
☎ 296-2991
In the heart of downtown. Close to all amenities. Conference facilities.

Curry Mansion $$-$$$
511A Caroline Street
☎ 294-5349
A charming small inn which is beside the Mansion in Old Town. Offers pool and amenities at the Pier House Beach Club just round the corner.

Days Inn Key West $-$$
(MM 4)
3852 N Roosevelt Boulevard
☎ 294-3742
A comfortable inn with restaurant, pool, gift shop, and 18 suites with full kitchens.

Deja Vu Clothing Optional Resort $$-$$$
611 Truman Avenue
☎ 292-9339
Facilities include patio res-

taurant, pools, spa and sauna, steam cabinet, massage room, fitness rooms and personal exercise regimes.

Eaton Lodge $$
511 Eaton Street
☎ 292-2170
Comfortable traditional inn in lovely tropical gardens, close to all amenities.

El Patio Motel $
800 Washington Street
☎ 296-6531
Small, comfortable budget accommodation with pool, close to all amenities.

Fairfield Inn by Marriott $$ (MM 2)
2400 N Roosevelt Boulevard
☎ 296-5700
Bayside with pool, bar and close to attractions and beaches.

Gardens Hotel $$-$$$
526 Angela Street
☎ 294-2661
In Old Town set in gardens with pool, hot tub, bar, continental breakfast.

Hampton Inn $$ (MM 2)
2801 N Roosevelt Boulevard
☎ 294-2917
Gulfside with pool, sunset deck bar, heated jacuzzi and continental breakfast.

Harborside Motel and Marina $-$$
903 Eisenhower Drive
☎ 294-2780

Pool, boat dock and marina, charter boats.

Hilton Key West Resort & Marina (B&B) $$$
245 Front St
☎ 294-4000
Luxury resort in the Old Town. Key West is only AAA Four Diamond Resort.

Holiday Inn Beachside $$-$$$
3841 N Roosevelt Boulevard
☎ 294-2571
On the Gulf with restaurant, bar, large pool, whirlpool, watersports, diving, gift shop and floodlit tennis. 50 foot (15m) fishing pier. Conference facilities.

Hyatt Key West $$-$$$
601 Front Street
☎ 296-9900 or
1-800-233-1234
This Hyatt is smaller and more intimate than most and is set in lovely tropical gardens. It offers 3 fine restaurants, 2 bars, pool, jacuzzi, gym, private beach, boat trips and sailing, watersports, mopeds, bikes, boutique. There are also snorkelling lessons and both aquarobics and aerobics. Conference facilities.

Hyatt Beach House Resort $$-$$$
5051 US highway 1
☎ 294-0059
The resort offers 74 two-bedroom 2-bathroom condos

with private bath and spa tub.

Island City House $$
William Street
☎ 294-5702 or
1-800 634-8230
A delightful guest house with apartment suites which include kitchen. There is a heated pool, jacuzzi and bikes, and a host of nearby eateries.

Key Lime Inn & Cottages $-$$
727 Truman Avenue
☎ 294-6222
Historic inn and private cottages with their own patios in tropical gardens with pool, in Old Town.

Key West Courtyard Bay View $-$$
3420 N Roosevelt Boulevard
☎ 294-5541
Formerly the Ramada with restaurant, bar, pool, volleyball and sports and miniature golf.

Key West International Hostel $
718 South Street
☎ 296-5719
Budget dormitory accommodation in Old Town, evening barbecues, bike hire and snorkelling trips.

La Mer Hotel $$
506 South Street
☎ 296-5611

A lovely old Conch guesthouse with porch and rocking chairs overlooking the ocean.

Mahogany House $-$$
812 Simonton Street
☎ 293-9464
Delightful cottage in Old Town. Beach, pool and health club membership and jacuzzi.

Marquesa Hotel $$-$$$
600 Fleming Street
☎ 292-1919 or
1-800-869-4631
Charming small hotel in historic 1844 house, with lovely rooms, pool and the excellent Cafe Marquesa restaurant. Good value.

Ocean Key Resort and Marina $$-$$$
Zero Duval Street
☎ 296-7701
Lovely location where the Atlantic Ocean meets the Gulf of Mexico, which explains its unusual address, with luxury suites and offering grill and raw bar, pool and sunset pier. Conference facilities.

Ocean Breeze Inn $$
625 South Street
☎ 296-2829
Great location in the Old Town with pool, patio and tropical gardens.

Palms Hotel $$-$$$
820 White Street
☎ 294-3146
In the heart of the historic district in a beautifully re-stored Victorian house, with tropical gardens, pool, cafe and bar. Meeting rooms.

Pegasus International $-$$
501 Southard Street
☎ 294-9323
Good value in the heart of Old Town in Art Deco hotel with sundeck.

Pier House $$$
1 Duval Street
☎ 296-4600 or
1-800-327-8340
A large luxury waterside hotel set in large gardens with its own private beach. Dine in the famed Pier House Restaurant with its fabulous wine list, or enjoy the sunset from the Old Havana Docks Sunset Lounge, where Jimmy Buffet started his musical career. There is also an alfresco cafe and bistro, bars, pool, sauna and health club, private beach and boutique. Conference facilities.

Pilot House
414 Simonton St
☎ 294-8719
Luxury guesthouse in a historic mansion. Clothing optional pool and spa set in lush gardens.

Quality Inn Resort $$
(MM 2), 3850 N Roosevelt Boulevard,
☎ 294-6681
Bayside with pool.

Santa Maria Motel $-$$
1401 Simonton Street
☎ 296-5678
Comfortable hotel built round courtyard with pool. There is a small restaurant.

Sheraton Suites Key West $$-$$$
2001 S Roosevelt Boulevard
☎ 292-9800
An all suite oceanside hotel offering complimentary full American breakfast. large pool. Conference facilities.

South Beach Oceanfront Motel $$
508 South Street
☎ 296-5611
Small, comfortable motel next to a small beach. There is a pool and it is a great place to watch those sunsets.

Southern Cross Hotel $
326 Duval Street
☎ 294-3200
A comfortable no-frills down-town motel close to all amenities.

Southwinds Motel $-$$
1321 Simonton Street
☎ 296-2215
In Old Town with pool, secluded courtyard and close to beach and all amenities.

Fact File

Travelodge & Suites Bayside $$-$$$
3444 N.Roosevelt Blvd
☎ 296-7593
A 64-room and suite resort overlooking the Bay at the southern most tip of the US.

Wicker Guesthouse $
913 Duval Street
☎ 296-4275 or
1-800-545-3907
A complex of 4 restored Conch houses with use of kitchen. Boat trips available.

Wyndham Casa Marina Resort $$$
1500 Reynolds Street
☎ 296-3535 or
1-800-228-9290
This historic landmark Old Town building was originally built by Henry Flagler as the Key West terminus of the Overseas Railroad. Built in Spanish Renaissance-style, its massive beachfront, has played host to scores of filmstars, politicians and celebrities over the years. It offers 311 luxury rooms on 1,100 feet (33m) of private oceanfront with restaurant, heated pool, giant jacuzzi, floodlit tennis, fishing, sailing, boat trips, cycles and mopeds, watersports, games room, fitness and health centre, grand ballroom and boutiques. Extensive conference facilities.

Bed and breakfast accommodation

Key West has a large number of excellent bed and breakfast establishments offering great value for money and all the comforts of home. For a full list contact the Greater Key West Chamber of Commerce. Some of the more outstanding b&bs include:

The Artist House $$
534 Eaton Street
☎ 296-3977

Casa Alante Guest Cottages $-$$
1435 S Roosevelt Boulevard
☎ 293-0702

Center Court $-$$
916 Center Street
☎ 296-9292

Conch House Heritage Inn $-$$
625 Truman Avenue
☎ 293-0020

Courtney's Place Historical Cottages and Inn $-$$
720 Whitmarsh Lane
☎ 294-3480

Island City House $$-$$$
411 William Street
☎ 294-5702

Lime House Inn $$
219 Elizabeth Street
☎ 296-2978

Merlinn Guest House $-$$
811 Simonton Street
☎ 296-3336

Fact File

Pilot House Guest House $$
414 Simonton Street
☎ 294-8719

The Pines $-$$
521 United Street,
☎ 296-7467

Simonton Court Historic Inn $$-$$$
320 Simonton Street
☎ 294-6386

Vacation homes and condo rental with reservation services

AA Accommodation Centre
☎ 296-7707

A Key West Information Station
☎ 293-0011

Accent on the Beach
☎ 296-9298

Accommodations Key West
☎ 294-6637

Accommodations Tan Keys
☎ 451-1013

All Florida Keys property Management
☎ 294-8877

Bassett Real Estate
☎ 296-8857

Beach Club Brokers
☎ 294-8433

Beachfront Condo
☎ 294-5283

Casa Buena Honeymoon Cottages
☎ 296-7559

Century 21 All Keys
☎ 294-4200

Coconut Beach Resort
☎ 294-0057

The Colony
☎ 294-6691

I Love Key West Reservation Center
☎ 294-4265

Key West Beach Club/ Harbor Lodge
☎ 294-8433

Key West Discovery
☎ 294-7713

Key West Realty
☎ 294-RENT

Rent Key West Properties
☎ 1-800-833-RENT

Sara Cook Realtor
☎ 294-8491

Fact File

AIRPORTS

Miami International Airport
☎ 876-7000

Marathon Airport
☎ 743-2155

Key West International Airport ☎ 296-7223

Sugarloaf Key Airstrip
☎ 745-2217

AIRLINES

American Eagle
☎ 1-800-433-7300

ComAir (Delta Connection)
☎ 1-800-354-9822

USAir Express
☎ 1-800-428-4322

Gulf Stream Airlines
☎ 1-800-992-8532/294-1421

Private Charter companies

Cape Air
☎ 1-800-352-0714

Ft. Jefferson Seaplanes
☎ 743-1900

Island Aeroplane Tours
☎ 264-8687

Key West Seaplane
☎ 294-6978

Vintage Charter
☎ 1-800-U-FLY-DC3

ALCOHOL

You must be 21 years old to purchase or consume alcohol in Florida. Do not be offended if you are asked to prove your age. You can enter lounges and bars serving alcohol if you are 18, but you must stick to soft drinks.

BABYSITTING

Most hotels and resorts offer baby sitting facilities, and there are also registered baby sitters services that will send baby sitters to your hotel room or villa, or take the children off your hands during the day. Most hotels and resorts also have special events and areas for children, from infants to teens, with trained staff to supervise them.

BANKS

Banks are usually open Monday to Friday from 9am to 3pm, although some stay open to 4pm. Automatic tellers which offer 24-hour access to cash are widely available. The following are the banks' main offices on the Keys:

Barnett Bank, Key West
☎ 292-3860
First National Bank, Marathon ☎ 743-9444
First State Bank, Key West
☎ 296-8535
First Union Bank, Key West
☎ 292-6600

Nations Bank, Marathon
☎ 743-4121
Republic Security Bank,
Islamorada
☎ 664-5247
TIB Bank, Key Largo
☎ 451-4660

BICYCLES

Cycling is a great way of exploring the Keys, and cyclists are well catered for. Cycling has two advantages, the countryside is flat, and you are more likely to get into the laid-back Florida Keys lifestyle by gently pedalling around.
There are many cycle rental shops, and cycle stands are provided throughout the Keys where you can leave your locked bike while you go to the beach, shop or eat.

BUS

Greyhound Miami	☎ 871-1810
Marathon	☎ 743-3488
Big Pine Key	☎ 872-4022
Key West	☎ 296-9072
Key West City Bus Terminal	☎ 296-8165

CAMPING / RECREATIONAL VEHICLES

RVs* pack the roads and campgrounds on the islands during the high season. RVs do offer high levels of accommodation with the added advantage that if you get tired of the scenery, you can always drive a few miles further up the road.

* For Overseas Visitors

RVs are recreational vehicles and trailers are motorised caravans and caravans.

Campgrounds and RV parks, which are found along the length of US1, are equipped to a high standard, with electricity and water hook-ups, on-site shops, restaurants, bars, pool and club house, as well as many other facilities.

Off-road camping is not permitted. Reservations are recommended during the winter 'high' season. For more information contact the Florida Campground Association, 1638 N Plaza Drive, Tallahassee, Fl 32308-5323 ☎ (904) 656-8878. There are campgrounds at:

UPPER KEYS

America Outdoors
(MM 97.5)
97450 Overseas Highway,
Key Largo
☎ 852-8054

Bluefin Rock Harbour Marina & RV Park
(MM 97.5)
Key Largo
☎ 852-2025

Calusa Camp Resort
(MM 101.5)
325 Calusa Road,
Key Largo
☎ 451-0232

Florida Keys RV Resort
(MM 106)
US1, Key Largo
☎ 1-305-451-6090

John Pennekamp Coral Reef State Park (MM 102.5)
US1, Key Largo
☎ 451-1202

Key Largo Kampground and Marina (MM 101.5)
Key Largo
☎ 451-1431

Kings Camp
103620 Overseas Highway
Key Largo
☎ 451-0010

MIDDLE KEYS

Estes Fishing Camp
Islamorada
☎ 664-9059

Gulfstream Trailer Park and Marina (MM 49)
Marathon
☎ 743-5619

Jolly Roger Travel Park
(MM 59.2)
US1, Grassy Key
☎ 289-0404 or
1-800-995-1525

Kampgrounds of America (KAO)
Fiesta Key (MM 70)
Long Key
☎ 664-4922

Key RV Park (MM 50.5)
Marathon
☎ 743-5164

Knight's Key Park (MM 47)
Marathon
☎ 743-4343

Lions Lair Travel Park
Rt.2, Marathon
☎ 289-0606

Long Key State Park
(MM 67.5)
Long Key
☎ 664-4815

133

Fact File

* For
Overseas
Visitors

Marathon Trailerama
☎ 743-6962

Outdoor Resort of America
(MM 66)
Long Key
☎ 664-4860

Pelican Trailer Park
Marathon
☎ 289-0011

Ocean Breeze RV Park & Marina
(MM 47.8)
Ocean side
Marathon
☎ 743-6020

BIG PINE KEY AND
LOWER KEYS

Bahia Honda State Park
(MM 37)
Big Pine Key
☎ 872-2353

Big Pine Key Fishing Lodge
(MM 33)
Big Pine Key
☎ 872-2351

Bluewater Key RV Resort
(MM 14.5)
☎ 1-800-237-2266

Breezy Pines RV Park
(MM 30)
Big Pine Key
☎ 872-9041

Brothers By The Bay RV Park
(MM 28.5)
Little Torch Key
☎ 872-2449

Castaways RV Park
(MM 30)
Big Pine Key
☎ 872-9710

Efficiencies-Park Models
Lazy Lakes (MM 19.5)
Sugarloaf Key
☎ 745-1079

Geiger Key RV Park and Marina
(MM 10.5)
County Road
☎ 296-3553

Halcyon Beach Trailer Park
(MM 31)
Big Pine Key
☎ 872-4601

Howards Haven Park
(MM 31)
Big Pine Key
☎ 872-9344

Lazy Lakes Resorts
(MM 19.5)
Sugarloaf Key
☎ 745-1079

Paradise Island Park
(MM 31.5)
Big Pine Key
☎ 872-4969

Royal Palm RV Park
(MM 31.5)
Big Pine Key
☎ 872-9856

Saddlebunch RV Park
Sugarloaf Key
☎ 745-3929

Sea Horse Campground
(MM 31)
Big Pine Key
☎ 872-2443

Sugarloaf Key KOA
(MM 20)
Summerland Key
☎ 745-3549

Sunshine Key Camping Resort and Marina
(MM 38)
Big Pine Key
☎ 872-2217

Venture Out Park
(MM 23)
Cudjoe Bay
Summerland Key
☎ 745-3340

KEY WEST

Boyd's Key West Campground
Maloney Avenue
Key West
☎ 294-1465

Jabour's Trailer Court
233 Elizabeth Street
Key West
☎ 294-5723

Leo's Campground
3236 Suncrest Road
Stock Island
☎ 296-5260

CAR RENTAL COMPANIES

Alamo
☎ 1-800-327-9633/
Key West 294-6675

Avis
☎ 1-800-331-1212/
Marathon Airport 743-5428/
Key West 296-8744

Budget
☎ 1-800-727-0700/
Marathon 743-3998/
Key West 294-8868

Dollar
☎ 1-800-421-6868/
852-4760/
Key West 296-9921

Duncan's Daily Rentals
Key West
☎ 296-6547

Enterprise
☎ 451-3998/664-2344/
Key West 292-0220

Hertz
☎ 1-800-654-3131/
Key West 294-1039

National
☎ 1-800-227-7368

Thrifty
☎ 1-800-367-2277/
Key Largo 852-6088/
Marathon 743-9289/
Key West 296-6514

Tropical Rent A Car
Key West
☎ 294-8136

Value Rent A Car
Marathon
☎ 743-6100
Key West
☎ 296-7733

CLOTHING AND PACKING

Pack light and wear light. The Keys are one of the few destinations where you can get away with a single piece of carry-on luggage if you are flying. Unless you are staying in a very smart resort, or like dressing up for dinner, T-shirts and shorts suit most people during the day, with slacks or jeans, and a casual shirt or blouse, ideal for balmy evenings. Sandals are fine for around the pool and beach (they are sometimes essential because the sand can literally get too hot to walk on with bare feet). If you plan to spend time walking, pack a comfortable pair of shoes or trainers.

Although the temperature drops a few degrees after sundown, most visitors still find it warm, even on winter evenings, but a light jumper is advisable if only to cope with the icy blast from the air conditioning. You will need swimwear, sunglasses and hat. The sun is deceptively strong, especially if there is a cooling sea breeze, and sunglasses not only help you see better in the glare, they will protect your eyes from harmful rays. You only have to spend a little time in Florida to appreciate how useful a baseball cap is.

CURRENCY *

The American dollar comes in denominations of $1, $2 (very rare), $5, $10, $20, $50 and $100. In practice, it is not a good idea to have the higher denomination bills and some establishments will not accept them. Always keep a few $1 bills handy for making up tips.

The dollar is divided into cents with the following coins: 1c (penny), 5c (nickel), 10c (dime) and 25c (quarter). There are 50c and $1 coins but these are rarely found in circulation.

Most major credit cards are widely accepted, particularly American Express, Diners Club, Visa and Mastercard. There may be problems occasionally in submitting foreign Access cards, but these are usually overcome if you point out that it is part of the Mastercard network.

There is little point in taking all your credit cards with you, so pick one or two that will be most useful, or allow you the greatest credit, and leave the rest at home in a secure place.

If taking traveller's cheques, make sure they are dollar cheques, which can be handed over in lieu of cash in most places. American Express can be contacted round the clock on ☎ 1-800-528-4800.

DISABLED

Florida leads the world in the provision of facilities for the handicapped. By law, all public buildings, National and State Parks must provide access facilities for the handicapped, and most hotels, resorts and attractions mirror this with superb access and facilities. There are also special provisions for the totally or partially blind or deaf. Many of the major car rental companies can provide specially adapted cars and vans with special controls, if given advance notice. There is a very useful booklet, *Florida Services Directory for Physically Challenged Travellers*, which lists relevant associations and facilities throughout the state. It is available from the Florida Department of Commerce Warehouse, 126 Van Buren Street, Tallahassee, Fl 32399-2000 ☎ (904) 487-1465.

DIVING

DIVE SITES

Key Largo	Grecian Rocks, Molasses, Pickles, Benwood, Elbow and French wreck sites, Spiegel Grove.
Islamorada	Davis Ledge, Conch, Wall, Spanish Plate Fleet wreck site, Alligator Reef, Pickles Reef, The Eagle.
Marathon	Adelaide Baker, Sombrero Reef, Coffin's Patch, The Thunderbolt.
The Lower Keys	Looe Key, Delta Shoals, Aquanaut wreck, Adolphus Busch Sr. wreck.
Key West	Sambo Reefs, Sand Key, Cottrell Reef, Joe's Tug, Ten Fathom Ledge, Cayman Salver and Kedge Ledge.

Fact File

* For
Overseas
Visitors

DIVE SHOPS AND CENTRES

This is just a small selection from the hundreds of dive shops and operators in the Florida Keys.

ISLAMORADA:

Holiday Isle Dive Shop
☎ 664 - DIVE

Lady Cyana Divers
☎ 664-8717

Rainbow Reef Dive Center
☎ 664-4600

Bay & Reef Company
☎ 393-0994

Conch Republic Divers
☎ 800-274-DIVE

KEY LARGO:

American Diving Headquarters
Key Largo
☎ 451-0037

Amy Slate's Amoray Dive Center
Key Largo
☎ 451-3495

Dual Porpoise Charters
Key Largo
☎ 394 - 0417

Dixie Divers
Key Largo,
☎ 453-9588 or
1-800-860-DIVE

Horizon Divers
Key Largo
☎ 453 - 3535

It's A Dive
Key Largo
☎ 453-9881

Ocean Divers
Key Largo
☎ 451-1113

Scuba-Do
Key Largo
☎ 522 - 1271

KEY WEST:

Dive Key West
☎ 296-3823

Dixie Divers
Key West
☎ 294-1111 or
1-800-860-DIVE

Get Wet
☎294-7738

Southpoint Divers
☎ 292-9778

Subtropic Dive Center
☎ 296 - 9914

LOWER KEYS:

Barnacle Dive
☎ 872 - 3298

Looe Key Reef Resort & Dive Center
☎ 872 - 2215

MARATHON:

Sombrero Reef Explorer
☎ 743-0536

Aquatic Adventures
☎743-2421

Fact File

Fantasea Divers
☎743- 5422

Marina at Hawk's Cay
Marathon
☎ 743-7000

Marathon Dive and Sport Center
☎ 289-2143

DRIVING ON THE KEYS *

Driving in Florida is a pleasure once you have got used to driving on the right hand side of the road and familiarised yourself with traffic signs and so on.

A valid driving license is needed by anyone wishing to rent a car in Florida, and you must be **21 years of age** or over.

Anyone planning to spend a lot of time in the state, may be well advised to get a Florida driving license, which is valid throughout the USA. You can usually walk into a driving test centre and join the queue to take the written and practical exam, providing you have proof of identification such as a birth certificate.

Many overseas automobile clubs are affiliated with the American Automobile Association (AAA), and proof of membership of one of these, entitles you to a range of services, including breakdown assistance, free maps and discounts for car rental, hotels and many attractions.

Because of the lower speed limits, wider roads and generally good lane discipline, foreign drivers should have no problems. It also helps if you can remember that **even-numbered roads** generally run east to west, while **odd-numbered highways** usually run north to south.

Normally if you want to get from A to B in a hurry, you use the Interstate.

In the Keys, you have to use US1 to get anywhere. It runs from Key West through all the Keys, and then north to Van Buren in Maine and the border with New Brunswick, Canada. Interstates have maximum speed limits of 55mph (88kph), except in some rural areas where it increases to 65 or 70mph (104 or 112kph). Interstates also often have minimum speed limits, usually 40mph (64kph). Resorts, beaches and attractions are reached from feeder roads from the US1.

Fact File

* For
Overseas
Visitors

ACCIDENTS

If you are involved in any road accident, exchange particulars with other drivers and get the names and addresses of any witnesses.

You must report to the police any accident that involves personal injury, or significant damage (anything other than a minor bump). Never admit liability or say 'I'm sorry', which may be taken as an admission of responsibility.

   * **Some insurance companies will not honour a policy if a driver has admitted liability.**

If you are driving a rented car, notify the rental company as soon as possible.

Important

If people are injured, no matter how hard it seems, leave medical assistance to those who are qualified to administer it.

   * **If you try to help and something goes wrong, you could face a massive bill for damages.**

RULES OF THE ROAD

· Always drive on the right and pass on the left.
· Buckle up because seat belts are compulsory
· Observe speed limits: 55-70mph (88-112kph) on highways, 25-40mph (40-64kph) in urban areas, and 15mph (24kph) in school zones.
    There are on-the-spot fines for speeding, and if you are caught going too fast, you could spend a night in jail.
    If stopped for speeding, don't pay the police officer, but pay fines direct to the relevant Clerk of the Court. Handing money to the police officer might be mis-interpreted as a bribe.
· Report all traffic accidents.
· If a school bus stops with its flashers on, traffic in both directions must stop while children get on or off. Traffic can only move when the bus moves off. The only exception is when oncoming traffic is separated from the bus by a central reservation, in which case it can proceed.
· Do not park near a fire hydrant. You will be fined and may be towed away.
    When parking at night, choose a spot that is well lit and, ideally, in a busy area. Lock all doors and make sure anything of value is out of sight.

- Always give way to emergency vehicles.
- U-turns are legal in Florida unless there is a sign to the contrary.
- When it starts to rain, turn your headlights and wipers on and reduce your speed.
- Do not pick up hitch-hikers.

Renting a car

It is usually cheaper to arrange your car rental through your travel company, or as part of a fly-drive package.

Although it is optional, you are strongly advised to have **Collision Damage Waiver** (CDW), and it is often cheaper to pre-pay this as well.

If flying into Miami, the rental companies are situated on the airport or a short drive away. If off the airport, courtesy buses shuttle to and from the car pick-up point.

At the car rental check-in, hand over your driving license, proof that you are 21 or over (passport) and your pre-paid voucher if you have one. You will be asked for an address where you will be staying, and if you are touring, give the hotel or motel where you will be staying on the first night. If paying by voucher, you will also be asked for a credit card to pay for incidentals such as airport tax, additional drivers and so on.

When you check in, do not be persuaded to upgrade or take out unnecessary insurance. Be sure you understand what they are trying to sell you.

Cars available range from economy models to limousines, and some rental companies will urge you to upgrade because they have run out of vehicles in the category you ordered. If you upgrade, they will charge you for a bigger car, if you refuse, they will be obliged to give you a bigger car at their expense. Car rental companies are listed on page 135.

Electric Cars can be rented at a number of locations. Two and four seaters are available from two hours to several days.

DRINK DRIVE LAWS

Driving under the influence of alcohol or drugs is a very serious offence in the Keys – even having an open container of alcohol in a car is illegal, and it is just not worth the risk of drinking and driving.

If convicted, the penalties are very severe, including imprisonment and vehicle confiscation. Driving under the influence of drugs is also a serious crime and you will probably end up in prison.

BREAKING DOWN

If you break down in a rural area, move across on to the hard shoulder, lift the bonnet (hood), and then get back into the vehicle, lock the doors and wait for help. If it is at night, you must use your emergency flashers. Police cars cruise the highways and will come to your aid.

If there is an emergency phone on the road, use that to call for assistance. If a member of an overseas motoring organisation affiliated to the AAA, you can ring toll free ☎ 1-800-AAA-HELP. If driving a rental car, notify them as soon as possible so that a replacement can be provided.

FILLING UP WITH GAS (PETROL)

All cars now run on unleaded fuel, but getting fuel can be confusing as pumps operate in a number of different ways. Read the instructions on the pump. Usually the nozzle has to be removed and then the bracket it rests on is moved into an upright position to activate the pump.

Some filling stations require pre-payment, some accept credit cards which can be inserted into the pump which then gives a receipt, some stations will only accept cash, and others charge more for fuel paid for by credit card.

Gas and diesel are often available at the same filling point. Do not get them confused.

142

ELECTRICITY *

Electrical appliances operate on a 110 volt, 60 cycles alternating current. Plug adapters will be needed if bringing dual or universal voltage appliances from Europe. Electrical appliances designed for 220-240v will be damaged if used on this power supply.

EMBASSIES AND CONSULATES *

USA Embassies abroad
Australia
36th floor, Electricity House, Park and Elizabeth Streets
Sydney NSW 2000 ☎ 02-261-9200

Canada
1155 Saint Alexandra, Montreal, Quebec H22 122
☎ 514-398-9695

New Zealand
4th floor, Yorkshire General Building, CNR Shortland and
O'Connell, Aukland ☎ 09-303-2724

UK
5 Upper Grosvenor Street, London W1A 2JB
☎ 0207-499-7010

Foreign Embassies and Consulates in Florida
UK
1001 South Bayshore Drive, Miami

EMERGENCY TELEPHONE NUMBERS

Emergency services — **Police**, **Fire** and **Ambulance** dial 911
US Coast Guard ☎ 664-3141, 664-4404, 742-6388 and 292-8856. If that fails, **dial 0 for the operator**.
  * A round-the-clock toll-free help line for tourists in trouble on or driving to the Keys is ☎ 1-800-771-KEYS.
  Multilingual operators can provide a wide range of assistance, from giving direction to drivers who are lost to details about the nearest medical facilities or auto repair centers.

FISHING GUIDE

For information on fishing, species and catch sizes allowed, contact:

Department of Natural Resources,
Office of Fisheries Management & Assistance Services,
Mail Station # 240, 3900, Commonwealth Boulevard,
Tallahassee Fl 32399-3000
☎ (905) 922-4340

There are 225 species of gamefish off the Keys. Average sizes and best months for catching the various species are:

Amberjack   15 to 75lbs (7 to 34kg) January to May
Barracuda   7 to 35 lbs (3 to 16kg) year round
Bonefish   5 to 16 lbs (2 to 7.25kg) April to October
Cobia   20 to 90 lbs (9 to 40.5kg) November
                to April
Dolphin   5 to 60 lbs (2 to 27kg) March to November
Grouper   5 to 80 lbs (2 to 36kg) year round
King mackerel 8 to 70 lbs (3.6 to 31.5kg) September
                to May
Blue marlin   120 to 600 lbs (54 to 272.75kg) April
                to December
White marlin   45 to 85 lbs (20 to 38kg) May to
                December, permit 8 to 40lbs (3.6 to 18kg)
                April to June
Sailfish   15 to 90lbs (7 to 41kg) October to May
Shark   20 to 1,000lbs (9 to 450kg) year round
Snapper   1-20lbs (.45 to 9kg) year round
Snook   6 to 35lbs (3 to 16kg) year round
Tarpon   25 to 200lbs (11 to 90kg) March to July
Tuna   8 to 200lbs (3.6 to 90kg) October to Au-
gust
Wahoo   15 to 70lbs (7 to 32kg) October to July
Redfish   3 to 20lbs (1.3 to 9kg) July to December

See pages 96/97 for Fishing Calendar

GAMBLING

Holiday Casino Cruises offer day and evening gambling cruises, with live entertainment and buffet. *The Pair-A-Dice* cruise ship sails from Key Largo ☎ 451-0000, or pick up tickets at the Key Largo Holiday Inn.

INSURANCE *

It is absolutely essential to have adequate insurance cover. It is
a good idea to keep a photocopy of your insurance policy with
you, and keep the original in your room. While medical service
is first rate, it can be expensive, and awards in the court for
damages as a result of an accident can be astronomic.

IRRITATING INSECTS

Mosquitoes can be a problem almost anywhere. If they are
a problem in your room, burn mosquito coils or use one of
the many electrical plug-in devices which burn an insect
repelling tablet. Mosquitoes are not so much of a problem
on or near the beaches because of onshore winds, but they
may well bite you as you enjoy an open-air evening meal.
Use a good insect repellent, especially if you are planning
trips inland such as walking in the humid forests and wood-
lands. Fire ants are also found, and their bites can be very
irritating.

Sand flies can be a problem on the beach. Despite their
tiny size (they are known locally as 'no-see-ems') they can
give you a nasty bite. And, ants abound, so make sure you
check the ground carefully before sitting down. Otherwise
you might get bitten, and the bites can itch for days.

MARINAS

ISLAMORADA:

Bud n' Mary's
☎ 664-2461
Coconut Cove
☎ 664-0123
Treasure Harbor
☎ 852-2458

KEY LARGO:

Curtis Marina
☎ 852-5218
Garden Cove
☎451 - 4694

Key Largo Harbor Marina
☎ 451-0045
Molasses reef
☎ 451-9411
Rock Harbor
☎ 852-2025
Rowells
☎ 451-1821
Tavernier Creek
☎ 852-5854

KEY WEST

Oceanside Marina
☎ 294-4676

Sea Horse Marina
☎ 292-9880

Garrison Bight
☎ 294-3093

Geiger Key
☎ 296-3553

Key West Conch Harbor
☎ 292-1727

Land's End Marina
☎ 296-3838

Safe Harbor
☎ 294-9797

Sunset Marina
☎ 296-7101

LOWER KEYS

Sugar Loaf Lodge
☎ 745-3135

Dolphin Resort & Marina
☎ 800-553-0308

Cudjoe Gardens
☎ 745-9976

Truman Annex Marina
☎ 293-9378

MARATHON

Cpt. Hoob's Marina
☎ 743-2444

MEDIA

The largest local paper is the daily *Key West Citizen* ☎ 294-6641. Weekly papers include the *Free Press* ☎ 664-2266; *Island Life* ☎ 294-1616; *The Newspaper, Key West* ☎ 292-2108; *Reporter* ☎ 852-3216; *Solares Hill* ☎ 294-3602 and *The Islander* ☎ 293-8829. *Keynoter* ☎ 451-4960 is published twice weekly. The *Florida Keys Magazine* ☎ 451-4429, keeps you abreast of what is on and has interesting articles about the Keys, their people and history.

US national and international newspapers are readily available, although the latter are usually quite expensive.

Cable and satellite television normally mean a choice of 40-60 stations. The three national networks and their local associate stations are ABC (Channel 10 WPLG), CBS (WFOR Channel 4) and NBC (WCIX Channel 6), while CNN provides round-the-clock news. Local stations include Channel 33 and Channel 40 Key TV.

Local radio stations for weather, boating and fishing conditions include Key Largo area: WCTH 100.3FM ☎ 664-1003; WKLG 102.3FM ☎ 451-2085 and WFKZ 103.1FM ☎ 852-9085. Marathon area: WGMX 94.3FM, WAVK 106.3FM and WFFG 1300AM. Key West: WJIR 90.9, WEOW 92.5 FM,

WKRY 93.5FM, WOZN 98.7FM, WPIK 102.5FM, WWUS 104.7FM, WIIS 107FM and WKIZ 1500 AM.

Fact File

NIGHTLIFE

There is a wide range of evening entertainment from theatre and concerts to zany nightclubs and piano bars. You can dine out and enjoy live entertainment at many of the large hotels and resorts, and mingle with the natives in waterside bars and clubs. Many bars and restaurants have live music supplied by small groups or solo musicians. You can enjoy comedy or listen to jazz, country and western, hard rock or dance until the early hours. There is a strong Cuban influence to the music on Key West with rumba and samba, and a special rhythm known as the Conchtown beat, a mix of New Orleans jazz, blues and Caribbean calypso.

PHOTOGRAPHY

The intensity of the sun can play havoc with your films, especially if photographing near water or white sand. Compensate for the brightness. Otherwise your photographs will come out over-exposed and wishy washy. The heat can actually damage film so store reels in a box or bag in the hotel fridge if there is one. Also remember to protect your camera if on the beach, as a single grain of sand is all it takes to jam your camera, and if left unguarded, it might 'disappear'. Always make sure when buying film that its expiration date is still a long way off. There are many outlets offering one hour developing of film, and it is a good idea to get early films developed, to make sure they are coming out alright, and that your exposure meter readings are correct.

POLICE

Emergency dial 911
Cudjoe Key ☎ 745-3184
Key West ☎ 296-2424

Marathon ☎ 289-2430
Key Largo/Plantation Key
☎ 853-3211

POST *

* For
Overseas
Visitors

Many shops, hotels and resorts sell stamps but it is often advisable to avoid stamp machines which can work out more expensive. Post Offices can handle all your mailing requirements, and even sell you special packaging if you want to ship gifts back home.

A first class airmail letter to anywhere in the US costs 32c, a postcard 20c. A postcard to be sent airmail to the UK or mainland Europe needs a 40c stamp, and an airmail letter costs 60c.

US Mail Boxes are not immediately obvious but can be found in most shopping areas. They are painted blue and bear the US Mail logo. There is a handle which when pulled, reveals a tray in which mail is deposited. When the tray is closed, the mail falls down into the box and cannot be recovered. There are usually facilities in hotels and so on, for posting mail. There are post offices in Key Largo (MM 100), Tavernier (MM 91), Islamorada (MM 82), Marathon (MM 49), Big Pine Key (MM 30), and Key West in Whitehead Street.

PUBLIC HOLIDAYS, ANNUAL EVENTS AND FESTIVALS

January

> January 1 **New Year's Day**. Public holiday
> **Art Under the Oaks**, Tavernier (☎ 664-5241)
> **Arts in the Park**, Pennekamp Park, Key Largo
> **Fishermen of Florida Seafood Festival**, Plantation Key (☎ 664-5956)
> **Florida Keys Renaissance Faire**, Marathon (☎ 743-4386)
> **Fort Lauderdale to Key West boat race** (☎ 849-4644)
> **Key West Arts and Crafts Show**, Key West (☎ 294-5015)
> **Martin Luther King Day** (third Monday)
> **Monroe County Fair**, Key West (☎ 294-2587)
> **Seafood, Arts and Craft Festival**, Plantation Key

February

> **Annual Rotary Seafood Festival**, Marathon (☎ 743-5417)
> **Blessing of the Fleet**, Islamorada
> **Civil War Days**, Fort Taylor, Key West (☎ 292-6850)

Florida Keys Art League Craft Show, Marathon
(☎ 743-6253)
Grace Jones Children's Festival, Marathon (☎ 743-7845)
Key West House and Garden Tours, Key West
(☎ 294-9501)
Old Island Days Art Festival, Key West (☎ 294-1241)
Pigeon Key Art Festival (☎ 743-7664)
Presidents Day (Third Monday)
Treasure Village Art Show, Islamorada (☎ 852-0511)

March

Conch Shell-blowing Contest, Key West (☎ 294-9501)
Key Colony Beach Day, Key Colony Beach (☎ 743-4320)
Marathon Seafood Festival, Marathon (☎ 743-5417)
Rain Barrel Arts Festival, Islamorada (☎ 852-3084)
Robert Frost Poetry Celebration, Key West (☎ 296-3573)
Treasure Village Art Show, Islamorada (☎ 852-0511)

April

Conch Republic Independence Celebration, Key West
Miami to Key Largo Sailboat Race
Seven Mile Bridge Run, Marathon (☎ 743-8513)

May

Big Pine Key Founder's Day, Big Pine Key (☎ 872-2411)
Clearwater to Key West Yacht Race, Key West
(☎ 813-585-7695)
Memorial Day (last Monday)
Pirates in Paradise Festival, Marathon (☎ 743-4386)

June

Gay Arts Festival, Key West (☎ 294-8658)
Sombrero Reef Sweep, Marathon (☎ 743-2522)

July

Fourth of July Independence Celebrations, various
locations
Hemingway Days Festival, Key West (☎ 294-4440)
Star Spangled Event, Marathon (☎ 743-5417)
Underwater Music and Seafood Festival, Looe Key
Marine Sanctuary (☎ 872-2411)
Women Fest, Key West (☎ 294-4603)

Fact File

* For Overseas Visitors

August

Historic Seacraft Race and Festival (☎ 872-2411)
Lobster Rodeo, Marathon (☎ 743-5755)

September

Annual Florida Keys Poker Run (☎ 294-3032)
Key West Theatre Festival, Key West (☎ 292-3725)
Labor Day (First Monday)
Save a Turtle Picnic, Pigeon Key (☎ 664-8252)

October

Columbus Day (Second Monday)
Fantasy Fest, Key West (☎ 296-1817)
Goombay Festival, Key West (☎ 293-8898)
Indian Key Festival, Islamorada (☎ 664-4704)

November

Armistice-Veteran's Day November 11
Island Jubilee and Arts and Crafts Festival, Key Largo (☎ 451-4747)
Thanksgiving Day (last Thursday)
World Cup Offshore Power Boat Race (☎ 296-8963)

December

Christmas House Tour and Christmas By The Sea, Key West
Christmas Day December 25
Lighted Boat Parade, off Key Largo in Blackwater Sound
Lower Keys Chamber of Commerce Annual Island Art Fair, Big Pine Key, (☎ 872-3580).

SAFETY *

There is no evidence to show that holidaymakers face any greater risk in Florida than they do in other places world-wide, and the Florida Keys, in particular, have comparatively low levels of serious crime. It makes sense, however, to take a few basic sensible precautions.

Do not wave money about, wear as little jewelery as possible and keep money, credit cards and passport separate.

Before leaving the airport make sure you know where you are going and which route you are taking. The car rental company will supply you with a map and directions, and signposting from Miami airport has been much improved in the last few years. If it is very late and you are tired, consider taking a taxi to an airport hotel and stay overnight so that you can continue your journey the next day refreshed and in daylight.

If you are staying in a hotel or motel, use their safe or the in-room safe if there is one, for valuables such as jewelery, extra money, tickets and passports. Carry a photocopy of the ID page of your passport in case you are officially asked for identification.

When travelling in a car, keep the doors locked and the windows up, and when leaving the car parked, make sure there is nothing visible that might tempt a thief. Never sleep in the car overnight, always find a cheap hotel or motel. When parking your car at night, try to leave it in an area where there is good lighting.

Ask the hotel staff or your holiday courier if there are any areas to avoid, and make sure you do not stray into them, especially late at night. It really is quite safe to walk around, but there is always the outside chance of a bag snatcher, or someone trying to grab your video camera, so be careful.

If you are stopped or threatened, do not resist. Most thieves only want cash or easily disposable items, and most will make their getaway as soon as you hand them over. If you are robbed, report it to the police immediately. Report the theft of credit cards and traveller's cheques to the appropriate organisations, and if your passport is stolen, report it as soon as possible to your Embassy or Consulate. The photocopy of the ID page will speed up replacement.

If luggage or property is lost or stolen, report it to the police and relevant authority (airport, car rental company, hotel) as soon as possible. Get a theft report from the police, try and contact your insurance company for permission to replace any stolen items, and keep all receipts.

Health

There are no serious health problems although visitors should take precautions against the sun and biting insects such as sand flies and mosquitoes, both of which can ruin your holiday. Biting bugs tend to come out late in the afternoon. If bitten by any animal, wild or domestic, seek medical attention as rabies is endemic in Florida.

There are also some poisonous snakes and spiders, but their bites are rarely dangerous if treated promptly, and such bites are, in any case, uncommon. Other minor problem areas include one or two nasty species of wasps.

Be careful around coral and be alert for jelly fish and spiny sea urchins which are occasionally a problem at some times of the year.

Immunisation is not required unless travelling from an infected area.

Most hotels and resorts have doctors on call around the clock, and emergency dental treatment is also available at all times. There are also a number of walk-in clinics which provide emergency treatment, and if the situation is really serious, drive straight to the nearest hospital's emergency room. Procedures for payment vary, but if you have insurance, ring their information line and seek advice. It may be that you have to pay for treatment on the spot, in which case, make sure you get all receipts so you can reclaim on your insurance.

Pharmacies will make up valid prescriptions from mainland US doctors, but visitors from Europe are recommended to bring in prescribed medicines together with a covering letter from your doctor, in case they are not available on the Keys.

Hospitals

Marathon Fisherman's Hospital offers 24-hour emergency service (☎ 743-5533).

TAXES *

Sales tax causes a lot of confusion among foreign visitors who find they are being asked to pay more for goods than the amount printed on the price tag.

State sales tax is 6 per cent, and local authorities can levy their own additional county tax of up to 1 per cent. These are added automatically when you pay.

Most goods are subject to this sales tax, but groceries and medicines are exempt, as are services 'that do not involve the sale of a tangible item' ie legal and accounting services. Hotel taxes are additional to the sales tax.

TAXIS

Taxis are plentiful and reasonable, and are a sensible option if you want to wine and dine outside your hotel. They also offer a safe way of travelling around late at night. Taxi companies are listed below.

KEY LARGO

Jeff's Keys Chauffeur Service ☎ 451-4328

Kokomo Cabs
☎ 852-8888

Upper Keys Transportation
☎ 852-9533

ISLAMORADA

Crown Limousine
☎ 664-2524

MARATHON

Cheapo Taxis
☎ 743-7420

Island Taxi
☎ 664-8181

Overseas Transportation
☎ 743-8500

KEY WEST

Friendly Cab
☎ 292-0000

Keys Taxis
☎ 294-2595

Key West Water Taxi
☎ 294-5687

Maxi Taxis
☎ 296-2222

TELEPHONES *

The emergency number for police, fire and ambulance is 911

The area code for all the Keys is 305 followed by the seven-digit local number.

Area codes are only used when dialling between areas.

Direct dialling of calls, even international ones, is possible from hotels, motels and most public phone boxes. Local calls cost 25c.

For international calls, dial the international code 011 followed by the country code (ie 44 for the UK), followed by the area code less the leading zero, and then the local number.

Most public phone boxes have instructions on how to place and dial international calls. If paying by cash, you will need a stack of quarters, and it is easier to use your credit card or reverse the charge (make a collect call).

Fact File

Dial 411 for local directory inquiries, or the area code + 555-1212 for long distance numbers.

TIME AND DATES *

South Florida is in the Eastern Time Zone which is the same time as in New York and 5 hours behind Greenwich Mean Time (ie when it is 12 noon in London it is 7am in the Keys).

Daylight Savings Time comes into effect on the first Sunday of April when the clocks go forward one hour, and they go back one hour to standard time on the last Sunday in October.

Americans write abbreviated dates with the month first and then the day and year. So Christmas Day 1999 is written 12/25/99

TIPPING *

In restaurants tip 15 per cent, or higher if you have had exceptional service, unless a service charge is automatically added to your bill.

If there is an automatic service charge and you do not think the service was good, complain and refuse to pay this charge.

Wages in the catering trade are low, and staff rely on tips to boost their take home pay. Tip porters $1 for every piece of large luggage carried, and it is customary to tip hotel maids $1 for each night they clean your room.

TOILETS *

Better known as the rest room, bathroom, men's room or ladies' room. Public toilets are found almost everywhere.

There are frequent rest areas with rest rooms along the main highway; you will find them in shopping malls, filling stations, restaurants, attractions, etc. Many stores even offer their own toilet facilities for shoppers.

Watch out for automatic flushing toilets which can take you by surprise!

TOURIST OFFICES

For information about the Florida Keys call 1-800-FLA-KEYS from the United States and Canada, or US 305-296-1552 from other countries. There are American tourist offices at the following addresses:

USA
US Travel and Tourism Administration, US Department of Commerce, Washington DC 20230 ☎ 0101-202-659-6000

UK
United States Travel and Tourism Administration, PO Box 1EN, London W1A 1EN ☎ 0207-495-4466

Canada
US Travel and Tourism Administration, Suite 602, 480 University Avenue, Toronto, Ontario M5G 1V2 ☎ 416-595-5082

TOURISM ENQUIRIES

Key Largo Chamber of Commerce
103400 Overseas Highway, Key Largo 33037. MM 106 ☎ (305) 451-1414 or 1-800-822-1088 Open Monday to Friday 9am to 5pm.

Florida Keys Visitor Center
MM 106, 105950 Overseas Highway. Open daily from 9am to 6pm.

Islamorada Chamber of Commerce
PO Box 915, Bayside, Islamorada 33036. MM 82.1 ☎ (305) 664-4503 or 1-800-FAB-KEYS

Visitor Center at MM 82.6
Bayside. Open Monday to Friday 9am to 5pm and at weekends from 9am to 2pm.

Greater Marathon Chamber of Commerce
12222 Overseas Highway, Bayside, Marathon 33050. MM 53.5 ☎ (305) 743-5417 or 1-800-842-9580

Visitors Center at MM 53.5
Open daily from 9am to 5pm.

Fact File

* For Overseas Visitors

BIG PINE KEY AND LOWER KEYS

Area Chamber of Commerce
PO Box 430511,
(MM 31) Big Pine Key
33043-0511
☎ (305) 872-2411 or
1-800-872-3722.
Visitors Center open Monday to Friday 9am to 5pm, Saturday 9am to 3pm.

KEY WEST

Greater Key West Chamber of Commerce
402 Wall Street,
PO Box 984,
Key West 33041
☎ (305) 294-2587 or
1-800-LAST-KEY

The Visitor Centre at 416 Fleming Street
Open daily 8.30am to 5pm.

WATER *

Note: Drinking water from the tap is perfectly safe, although bottled mineral and distilled water is widely available.

WEDDINGS *

You can get married in church, at historic monuments, at sunset, at sea or even under it if you are keen divers.

Many hotels offer wedding planners and honeymoon packages. You can download more information from the Florida Keys and Key West website: www.fla-keys.com.

WEIGHTS AND MEASURES *

Americans still use the Imperial system of weights and measures, although metric measures are becoming more common.

Road distances are always in miles while gas (petrol) can be in either gallons or litres, or both.

Liquid measures differ between America and Britain. One US gallon = 0.833 Imperial Gallons = 3.8 litres.

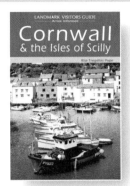
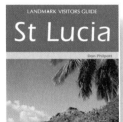

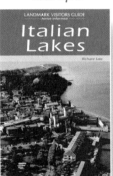

A

Accommodation 104
Airlines 131
Audubon House 80

B

Bahama Village 80
Bahia Honda Key 63
Beaches 19
Before you go 102
Big Pine Key 64
Blue Hole 65

C

Camping/Recreational
Vehicles 132
Canoeing 24
Car Hire Companies
135
Clothing and Packing
136
Conch Key 51
Conch Republic 76
Crane Point Hammock
56
Crawl Key 52
Cudjoe Key 67
Currency 136
Customs 103

D

Diving 24, 137
Dolphin Research
Center 52
Dolphins Plus Research
Center 33
Donkey Milk House
81
Drink Drive Laws 142
Duck Key 51

E

East Martello Fort
Museum 81
Embassies and
Consulates 143
Ernest Hemingway
Museum 83

F

Fat Albert 68
Fishing 25
Fishing Calendar 96,
97
Fishing guide 144
Flagler, Henry 13
Flora and Fauna 17
Florida Key's Children's
Museum 57
Florida Keys Wild Bird
Rehabilitation Center
35
Food and Drink 21
Fort Zachary Taylor 84

G

Gambling 144
Geography 7
Golf 26
Grassy Key 52

H

History 9
Holiday Inn Key Largo
Marina 33
Hurricane Monument
44
Hurricanes 16

I

Indian Key 46
Islamorada 39

J

John Pennekamp Coral
Reef State Park 29
Jules Undersea Lodge
28

K

Key Colony Beach 52
Key Deer 20
Key Deer National
Wildlife Refuge 65
Key Largo 27
Key Largo Hammocks
State Botanical Park
28
Key Largo National
Marine Sanctuary 33
Key Largo Undersea
Park 28
Key West 71
Key West Aquarium 87
Key West Cemetery 87
Key West Festivals 99
Key West Shipwreck
Historeum 89
Knight Key 52

L

Lignumvitae Key State
Botanical Site 45
Little White House
Museum 92
Loggerhead Key 68
Long Key 50
Looe Key National
Marine Sanctuary 67
Lower Keys 63
Lower Matecumbe
Keys 41

M
Mallory Market 92
Manchineel tree 18
Marathon 53
Marriott Casa Marina
  Resort 92
Media 145
Middle Keys 51

N
No Name Key 65

O
Old Seven Mile
  Bridge 57

P
Plantation Key 40
Public Holidays 148

R
Rainfall 16
Rules of the Road 140

S
Saddlebunch Keys 68
San Pedro Underwater
  Archaeological Park
  50
Shipwreck Museum 29
Shopping 22
Silver Palm Nature
  Trail 64
Snakes 20
Stock Island 73
Summerland Key 67
Sunshine Key 63

T
Tarpon Flats 44
Tavernier 35

Temperature 16
Tennis 26
The Dry Tortugas 90
Tipping 154
Turtle Kraals 98

U
Upper Matecumbe
  Keys 41

V
Vaca Key 53

W
Watersports 26
Watson's Hammock 67
Weather 16
Windley Key 40
Wrecker's Museum 98

Published by
Landmark Publishing Ltd,
Ashbourne Hall, Cokayne Avenue, Ashbourne,
Derbyshire DE6 1EJ England Tel: 01335 347349 Fax: 01335 347303
E-mail landmark@clara.net Web-site www.landmarkpublishing.co.uk

Published in the USA by
Hunter Publishing Inc,
130 Campus Drive, Edison NJ 08818
Tel: (732) 225 1900, (800) 255 0343 Fax: (732) 417 0482
Web site: www.hunterpublishing.com

3rd Edition
13 ISBN: 978-1-84306-210-3
10 ISBN: 1-84306 210-0

© Don Philpott 2006

British Library Cataloguing in Publication Data: a catalogue record for this
book is available from the British Library.

Print: Biddles Ltd., King's Lynn
Design: James Allsopp

Cover Pictures
Front: Smathers Beach, Key West
Back: The most southerly point in the USA, Key West

Picture Credits:
Don Philpott: all save for;
Florida Keys Tourist Development Council: 15 inset, 22, 27, 31T,
34M, 38, 51, 55, 71, 74, 82L, 82T, 95T, 106, 115, back cover
Department of Environmental Protection: 11T, 42M
Cheeca Lodge, Islamorada: 15
Sheraton Key Largo Resort: 34B
Laurel Canty, Dolphin Research Center, Grassy Key, Florida: 34T
Florida Department of Tourism: 83, **Pier House:** 86
Sheraton Suites Key West: 114B